Illustrations by Kinga Martin
Book Design by Kyla Korytoski

ISBN 978-1-7344269-0-8
Published by JJMacD LLC
jjmacdllc@gmail.com

Becoming JoJo MacBean

BY ANDREW PIGNATARE

FOREWARD

Although I had a decent business career, do not compare me to JoJo MacBean. We had a couple of similarities, but JoJo was far more intelligent than I. This novel, which is my first one, started with a dream I had in 1999. It took a long while to write because I owned a CPA firm that consumed much of my time. I worked on this novel on and off throughout the years. And then I really found more time to complete this project over the last five, working on a part-time basis.

I thought someday that I would write my first and only book about "How to achieve success owning your own business". But then the dream came along, and here we are!

I want to thank my beautiful wife, Terry Ann, for her loving support. Thanks to all my friends for keeping me motivated! And I need to especially thank my friends,who helped me bring this book to fruition: readers and editors, Fran, Chris, and Kay; illustrator Kinga, and formatter Kyla, and Rick of Pignatare and Sagan. I am grateful to you all.

And to my friend, Bob, who kept reminding me for three years that I needed to be a time millionaire, I say, "Guess what,! Because of you, I finally am!"

Andy

After all, the chief business of the American people is business... Cal Coolidge 1925

The history of America is the history of Wall Street... JoJo MacBean Jan. 1991

HARVARD COMMENCEMENT - May 2011

A man of sixty-five, dressed in a kilt with the MacBean tartan and sporran, stood at the podium on a warm spring day in May. He looked out on the faces in the audience and remembered how excited he had been to leave Harvard rather than go through two years more of sitting in a classroom when the world, the real world, was waiting for him to set it on fire. And here he now stood, receiving an honorary degree, and speaking to the graduates. The President of the University called him Joseph Joshua MacDyer MacBean, just as MacBean had asked him to. He was no longer a legal MacDyer, but legalities were mere pieces of paper compared to blood. He was a MacDyer down to his Scottish bones. He walked first to the President to receive his degree and found himself wondering why the honorary degrees were usually large silk lanyards holding a medal, unlike any other degree he'd ever seen. Then he walked to the podium and began his speech. He spoke so softly someone shouted, "Can't hear you". He began again.

"My name is JoJo MacBean. Most people call me just MacBean. When I tell people my story, I tell them it's all truth, even the parts that might not be true. I was born and raised, I conquered Wall Street, Wall Street conquered me, I lived a hobo life, I stole from dead people, and I made a comeback, as witnessed by my standing here before you today. Oh, I also had four wives. Not much else to tell about me except what I've learned along the way. It's nothing new, in fact, it's so very, very old, it seems strange that anyone ever has to repeat it. And yet they do. We do. I do. Over and over and over. Because we don't want it to be true. We want life to be simple, work to be simple, humanity to be simple. It's not and never will be.

My tale offers nothing new but will be added to the myriad of stories before it of men who did not understand the genuine treasures life could hold – if only they would understand what drove them to do the things they did, I mean really understand the why, not the what. I have told my story to many people, including my homeless buddies, my detective friends, and a few of my old business partners. And in the case of the detective friends, they told me their stories as well, so I might add them to mine. Of course, my wives heard a version that ended when each marriage did. It was one of the detective friends who suggested I should put all this down, just in case somebody might learn something from it. He also said it would give me something positive to do while I was in prison. I ended up not writing my book. My best friend, who also happens to be my life partner, wrote it based on the stories I told her. She loves me, so I worried that it might make me out to be more of a saint than I was, but when I read it, I knew I needn't have worried.

"The business of America is business" said Cal Coolidge. And he was right. But the business of you, students of 2011, is decidedly NOT business. Not ONLY business. I do not mean you shouldn't make money, and lots of it. But if you make becoming rich your number one reason for working, you will end up the poorest of the poor, for you will cease to be a human being. Money is a byproduct of your passionate endeavors, whatever they may be. Oh, by God, it's better to have money than not to have it. But it buys no time, it buys no love, it buys no understanding, it buys only nourishment of the body, not of the soul. It pisses people off that only a rich man ever says this. But only a rich man can know this with complete certainty.

Not much else for me to say. Good luck to you all. And please, go buy a copy of my book when it comes out; the back of the book has a list of the lessons I learned. I hope you learn them from reading the book, but if you're a knucklehead like me, you might need the list, too. And I thank you in advance for buying it because...well... I'm no longer a man with money to spare, even though I'm the richest man on earth."

In September, 1920, a bomb exploded on Wall Street killing thirty-eight people and injuring one hundred forty-three others. It was believed detonated by anarchists, though that was never proved. Sadly, it would not be the last explosion in the financial district. (1)

1

BORN & RAISED

1920 (b.1946) – 1964

The market began 1920 at 108 and ended 1964 at 874. [(2)]

Lonnie and Claire had lived in Elgin, Scotland since they'd been born very early in their new century, the 20th that is. Elgin, at the time, was the smallest town in Scotland. Like many Scottish towns, it was founded in the Middle Ages and had several cathedrals and castles that were built in the early days. It was also very poor. It was the land of the fertile soil with the Lossie River bordering the town and the climate good for crops and animals for much of the year. Many farmers lived there, but most of them barely eked out a living. Elgin had begun constructing roads and bridges in hopes of building up the commercial trade.

Lonnie's father, like many others, grew grains, potatoes, and turnips. There were also many pastures for grazing and much hay to be harvested. Lonnie started working at a few of the local farms at four years old, picking up odd jobs. In those hard times, most of the children began just as Lonnie had, helping their families from the time they could walk. It was a simple matter of survival.

Elgin also had some factory mill workers called balers. But Lonnie became a docker at the tender age of thirteen, thought to be one of the better jobs. Along with weavers of cloth, hat makers and beadsmen, who were licensed beggars, blacksmiths called nailors, and sawyers who worked in saw mills, they all worked long hours, but the reality was there was very little food to eat because of frequent famines and shortages. JoJo would remember his mum telling him that many a time a mum or dad ate little or nothing, so their children could be fed.

Scotland was also a land of many epidemics. People would sicken, die, and be buried before there was even time to make note of it somewhere. Almost half the death certificates issued listed the wrong cause of death. With twelve to sixteen people boarding in one room in the poorest parts of the towns, epidemics were a fact of life, or rather of death. The struggle seemed to reach back for centuries. The people of Scotland had begun to ask if there had ever been a time of plenty, a time when mothers did not lose many of their young children to sickness including milk being diluted with diseased water to stretch it further, and poor nutrition from the sheer lack of enough food. By the time Lonnie and Claire were born, shortly after the death of Queen Victoria, the Scotch emigration was in full swing. Most of those emigrants were dreaming of a new and better life in America, just as Lonnie and Claire would, until they could make it a reality.

Lonnie formally met Claire when he was eleven years old, and she was eight. Lonnie's dad also raised sheep, and Lonnie had been working on that farm for seven years. But the farm still couldn't provide more than a subsistence living. Claire lost her dad at a young age in a quarry accident. Her mum struggled to bring up three young ones by being a seamstress, a profession that Claire also learned at a very young age. In the days that Lonnie managed to make it to school, it was clear he'd set his cap for Claire.

When Lonnie turned thirteen, like many that age, he left

schooling behind and went to work full time for the family, tending sheep and farming, and picking up work whenever he could get it, loading and unloading cargo. Eventually, he ended up fulltime in the freight business. He started courting Claire when she was fourteen, with Claire's mum chaperoning. In 1919, after three years of bad weather that yielded poor crops, food once again became very scarce for both man and livestock. Once in a while, a wild rabbit or squirrel was caught for the dinner table to use in a stew, but, primarily, the Scots lived on potatoes and turnips. If they were lucky, an occasional glass of goat's milk graced their table along with the meal.

Twelve to sixteen hours a day, six days a week, families toiled with little to show for it in either money or food. Yet, young couples continued to marry, as did Lonnie, eighteen, and Claire, fifteen, in 1923. The groom was young and ambitious and badly wanted a better life for himself and his bride. Like many Scots, he kept talking about seeking a new opportunity for them in America. A few months before making the final decision, they talked to their dearest friend, Stuart Campbell, and his young bride, Amelia. Stu and Amelia also became excited about the opportunities in America. He thought he could learn more about his trade of shipbuilding and hoped to someday start his own business. In 1924, both young couples bid farewell to their families and to Scotland. Although young in years, all four had watched their parents struggle, had watched as crops failed, livestock perished, children died, and hope for a better future vanished over the Scotch moors. Yet they were ready to work as hard as ever. One might ask why, and it would be the same answer given throughout human history. It was their only hope to give their children the opportunities they never had.

When Lonnie and Claire arrived in New York City, they did not have many work skills, but they had an old-fashioned work ethic. Lonnie found work within days after arriving in New York City, loading and unloading freight as a dock worker, working ten to twelve hours a day and five hours on Saturday in the back-breaking work that paid the bills. Claire followed in her mum's footsteps as a seamstress. She would work independently from her flat, and she always had small jobs from people in the neighborhood. She didn't make a lot for her work, but she loved it. The money that she did make helped support the household expenses.

The Black Tuesday stock market crash of 1929 produced the Great Depression, during which half of all banks failed, and unemployment rose to 25%. Historians agree it lasted until 1939, and some argue its effects lingered significantly until 1941. (3)

In spite of the Depression, or perhaps because it made them all the more thrifty, if that were possible, within five years the MacDyers bought a very small two-bedroom house on the upper East Side. Many people of Scottish and Irish descent lived in that neighborhood, some in small houses, some in double-deckers, and some in flats. Claire kept their little home very neat. She loved the neighborhood, and she filled their home with little knick-knacks from Scotland, Ireland, Wales, and England that she sometimes received from her sewing clientele as thank-you gifts. She never told Lonnie, but she sometimes had to take the knick-knacks instead of any payment.

Times were still tough, the Depression continued to linger, and Claire had an understanding heart. She also knew she could always sell the knick-knacks, if needed. It was indeed a happy household. The MacDyers remained grateful their entire lives for the opportunity to own their own home, especially at a fairly young age. It only affirmed their good judgement in coming to America. They understood the value of a hard day's work and of saving one's money for the things that truly mattered. Scots through and through!

When the second World War began, Lonnie registered for the draft but was told his age would probably make it likely he would get a deferment if called. He was never called, but joined in the war efforts at home by helping to sell bonds, leading recycling drives, and serving on his company's committee to ensure dock workers stayed vigilant to report any suspicious activity. Claire used her scrap piles to make quilts to be sent to the soldiers overseas.

The couple's attempts at starting a family drifted further away each year, as Claire suffered four miscarriages. After a number of years, the miscarriages had stopped, but it seemed as though she simply was unable to conceive. Claire was secretly grateful, believing that any conception would only end in more tragedy. She channeled her efforts into working longer hours as a seamstress. Her skill at making a wardrobe out of practically anything began to spread beyond their neighborhood. In 1946, when Lonnie was forty-one and Claire thirty-eight, the doctor confirmed that Claire was pregnant. After twenty-three years of marriage, the MacDyers had another chance to become the parents they'd always prayed to be.

"Oh, he's a wee one, isn't he?" new dad Lonnie said to new mum Claire as she laid in bed with newly named Joseph Joshua MacDyer, swaddled next to her and named after both his grandfathers. He was born prematurely and weighed barely five pounds.

"The doctor says he's in perfect health". It wasn't the idle chat of new parents. The memories of miscarriages were never out of mind. They believed it was truly a miracle, and yet they never relaxed their guard against the tragedies that might befall a child. Their personal histories told them it was never safe to be complacent. And, yet, that same guardedness made them grateful, loving parents to their child. Lonnie and Claire had made an entirely new life in America based on a bond of trust in their ability to triumph over anything with hard work and love, and they would continue to do so. Here, now, was little Joseph Joshua to declare they were right in that.

"What will we call him, Lon? Joseph, Jo, Joseph Joshua, ooh, a mouthful there." said mum.

"How about just JoJo?"

"That's perfect, a little name for a little baby. We'll save the Joseph Joshua for when he's a man."

But destiny had a different idea in store for JoJo. When he was just three, the local priest said to him one Sunday morning "Aye, you're no bigger 'n a jelly bean", to which JoJo responded "I'm not a jelly bean! I'm a human bean!" to which Father Connery responded back, "Oh, so we're a human MacBean now are we?"

From that time on, he was called MacBean by everyone but his parents, who always called him JoJo, even well past his becoming a man. With a late high school growth spurt, he reached six feet, but the name was too ingrained by then. Soon after he reached twenty-one, he changed it legally to MacBean simply to avoid confusion as to who he was, for someone was always asking, "Who the hell's this MacDyer lad?"

MacBean's parents were always loving but also strict. They were also quite protective of him, probably more so because he was an only child and would always remain one. MacBean would struggle throughout his life with his early tendency to keep to himself, considering his parents to be his two best friends.

He was an average student in grammar school with the exception of his work ethic. That one thing set MacBean apart from the other children from a very early age. He never forgot that he was the son of Lonnie and Claire MacDyer and his dad would tell him "don't you never forget it neither"! It would become the key ingredient that made him the businessman he was, then and later. Always in overdrive mode, always ambitious, that was MacBean. His dad's work ethic, and his mum's business, enabled the family to achieve a middle-class life with plenty of food to eat and decent clothes thanks to mum's tailoring skills. It was a typical American success story. Oatmeal for breakfast, bread and cheese for lunch, and a piece of fish or meat along with a potato and some milk for supper. Claire also made homemade soups from the scraps left at the dinner table. There was always some fresh fruit on the table for snacking. But her specialties were the fruit pies or cobblers she'd make if any fruit were in danger of spoiling. Claire would sometimes accuse Lonnie of deliberately not eating the fresh fruit just so she would make a cobbler, an accusation he would never deny. Lonnie always said the family ate more in one or two days than he and Claire ate in a week back in Scotland. There was never any question for them that they had made the right decision in coming to America.

To say they were middle class was true. To say they were still frugal was an understatement. Claire saved the extra scrap materials from her tailoring, and, from those, she made all the family clothes. MacBean was noticeably the best dressed boy in the neighborhood. The whole family looked dapper and fashionable in the same materials as the most fashionable men and women on 5th Avenue!

But the clothes and his Scottish background didn't help him fit in with his school chums or in the neighborhood, never being considered an official part of the neighborhood gang. Most of the kids were better athletes than he even after his growth spurt, although he did play a lot of stickball, soccer, and marbles in spite of his early size challenge. MacBean was much smarter than any of them, although he didn't always demonstrate that in his school studies. He was more interested in learning on his own, being on his own, reading books at home or listening to Dad's stories about Scotland, or helping Mum make shortbread cookies on the rare occasions they could afford the extra butter. Yet, even though he was often left out of neighborhood games and sports, he never felt alone. That's not to say he didn't feel very different. That feeling would be with him for the rest of his life, in ways both positive and negative.

MacBean also had a decided gift for math. Some of the kids in the neighborhood thought he was weird because of this. Being well-dressed and a great student in math made him stand out in a way that seemed to irritate the other kids. Needless to say, along the way he got a few more black eyes than most of the other neighborhood kids. Even after he reached the Catholic high school out of the neighborhood, he couldn't say he had any real close friends.

The more the neighborhood gang avoided him, the more he seemed to escape by studying and excelling in the classroom in math. It began to give him confidence in other subjects that he hadn't cared much about before. But unlike math, he had to study hard on those subjects. Eventually he was making the honor rolls and becoming a top student. Still, most of the people he liked best and talked to most frequently were adults except for a few church friends from his regular Sunday attendance at Mass.

In 1930s New York City, over 1500 Jewish delis flourished. They offered a safe, social gathering place, especially for those who were not regular attendees at local synagogues. The delis also offered familiar food and what were initially thought to be "extravagant" meats. (4)

Once MacBean realized very early on that he was a natural businessman, his ambition grew by leaps and bounds. He got his first paying job at Bloomberg's Deli in Manhattan, Solomon

Bloomberg proprietor/owner, when he was ten, navigating the subways from home. Sol was the second generation; his father having opened it in 1923 with the help of Sol's grandparents who sent money from Germany to invest in getting the deli up and running. Mr. Bloomberg had told MacBean that every week his papa would say in Yiddish "Samdey, Got s vet", someday, God willing. But by the time the deli broke even, it was too late for the grandparents. That he had not sent for them before their disappearance, likely to the concentration camps, Sol's papa never got over, dying broken hearted, just after D-Day. But break-even it had, and Sol now owned a quite successful Jewish deli in the heart of the Wall Street district. It was known as the place for great food and even greater financial gossip. Bloomberg, himself, was a cheerful man who kept any sadness between himself and his God. MacBean thought he'd never met a man as cheery as Mr. Bloomberg. *And why not?* MacBean thought. A deli making good money, what would he have to be sad about?

Every time MacBean stepped into it, he marveled at the spotless black and white squares on the floor, the shiny chrome and laminate on the tables, and the deli cases – meats and chicken, lox and bagels, corned beef and pastrami, and – on and on. The meat locker in the back of the store was something strange and wondrous to a young boy, especially when Mr. Bloomberg would tell him ten times a day to remember that the meat locker has the lock on the outside! He'd say *mura habn*, the equivalent of "don't risk your life by going in when nobody knows you're in there". MacBean began there by sweeping and mopping the floors. While he was cleaning them, he'd listen to the stock brokers talk about the market. Hearing all of their stock market terminology generated a keen interest in MacBean. Is it any wonder he was considered a weird kid?! He began working for a nickel a day plus a thick deli sandwich. He was proud that he was carrying his share of the responsibility by saving on some weekly food costs by eating at the deli. In addition, he had a paper route plus a couple of other side businesses. He was a burgeoning young entrepreneur. Yet another activity the neighborhood kids didn't understand or appreciate, which only made them reaffirm that MacBean was as weird as they always thought. Lonnie asked his son, JoJo, about those side businesses, and JoJo would smile slyly and say "one is selling… uh, protection." Lonnie replied, "You mean, rubbers?!"

"Yes, Dad, you see there is a kid named Arthur who's about fourteen years old, stayed back three times. He's a bit short on brain power. His dad is a pharmaceutical rep, and among the supplies he sells to the pharmacies are boxes of condoms. Arthur sells me a gross for three dollars, and I sell them to high school and college kids."

"Are you making money, Son?"

"Oh yes, Dad. There are three condoms in a package and forty-eight packages in a gross. I sell one for a quarter or three for fifty cents.

"Don't ever let your mother know about this. Or, for Lord's sake, Father MacIntosh. And, I promise ye, if you're caught, I'll deny I knew. I'll have to Son, for the family's sake." And then Lonnie winked at his son.

For about three months, MacBean had made a killing, until his mother Claire found out. Of course, Lonnie also pretended to be upset, but MacBean convinced them that since he personally did not use them (and he didn't being just barely eleven) that it was only a money- making enterprise and not a sin. Even his mum seemed to take a sliver of pride in her son's get up and go, even while acting annoyed. He did, however, have to discontinue his dreams of a condom empire. But MacBean had taught Arthur how to run the business, and he continued to do quite well until his old man figured it out with an annual inventory. Unfortunately for Arthur, he couldn't claim not to be using them.

MacBean also knew an Italian kid, named Angelo, whose

nono made homemade Italian wine, kept in big wooden barrels. Angelo would tap the barrels for MacBean and give him a gallon of wine once or twice a week for one dollar per gallon. MacBean would then take empty three cent milk cartons, wash them out, and pour the wine into them, then take the cartons to the local high school to sell for fifty cents each at a seven dollar per gallon profit. Of course, after a while, he got caught doing that, too. Both enterprises taught MacBean about business, most importantly about finding a demand, selling a product or service to meet the demand, and making a profit doing it. Seemed surprisingly simple to MacBean.

It became a little less simple when Nick "Blackie" Blackstone arrived in the neighborhood. Nick's father, in spite of the waspy name, was connected to the mob, and Nick was following in his old man's footsteps by asking MacBean for a cut of every "game" he had going. MacBean refused. Nick said MacBean would be sorry. He refused again.

"How come you're not folding up like every guy my dad shakes down?" asked Nick.

"Because you're not going to beat me up."

"Says who?"

"Says me."

"And why's that, wise guy?"

"Because if we work together, we can make more."

"And just how do you figure that, genius?"

"Well, first of all, everybody calls me MacBean. Not wise guy, not genius, just MacBean. And secondly, if you treat me as a partner, I'll go on coming up with new ways to make us money. You treat me badly, I stop all of it, you make nothing."

"How's about I just beat you up, like you said?"

"OK, go ahead. It's a shame though. Two guys like us, could do very well, don't you think?"

Blackie stood pondering this, then extended his hand, which MacBean took in a handshake saying, "Partners. But not 50-50. I get 70, you get 30."

"I like you, MacBean. Tell you what. Our first game'll be 70-30. Our second game will be 60-40, and our third one, and all the rest, will be 50-50. Deal?"

"On one condition."

"What's that?"

"That you stop calling my businesses games. They're not games. They're well planned and well executed businesses. I, JoJo MacBean, am a businessman, not somebody who runs games. Deal?"

With another handshake Blackie and MacBean went into neighborhood business, including an errand service, hiking up to a posh Manhattan neighborhood and taking stuff from people's trash on trash day such as old trikes and toys and then reselling the items to second hand stores, and their most successful enterprise of selling shares in their other businesses. Blackie came up with the idea and would be the one to sell it to other kids and MacBean figured the numbers out. Blackie assumed it needed to be underhanded somehow, but MacBean explained that it wasn't necessary, the numbers themselves would make the profit. They would tell a kid that if he invested just a dollar, at the end of the year he'd get back a dollar and a quarter, then used that upfront dollar to expand and grow the business, then both Blackie & MacBean and the kid would end up with more money. MacBean kept track of how many kids each business could support since every business had a different level of possible expansion. It worked so well on the enterprises they used it with, that six months after they began Blackie said to MacBean, "You're wrong, MacBean. This is, too, a game."

MacBean stood still thinking on Blackie's remark when he responded, "if everybody wins, it's can't be a game, not like you mean. If we win but somebody loses, that's a game."

"No, ya dope, I don't mean a "game" game, like the numbers racket down at O'Reilly's place. I mean like a game you play, for fun."

"When you make money, it's always fun. But when you risk

money, that's not fun. Making it and risking it are two different things. Can't be a game if you risk losing."

"You're missing the point, genius. All I'm saying is that to you, all the planning you do, figuring out stuff with numbers, that's fun for you."

"Only if it works, Blackie, only if it works."

"No way, Mac & Bean, I seen you when you're working a plan out, ya look like a jack o lantern the way your face is lit up!"

"OK, have it your way." The next moment Blackie's ma walked into the yard the boys were in and said to Blackie to come into the house. MacBean had never seen a face like hers before, totally blank, eyes all red from crying. Blackie came by the MacDyer house that evening to tell MacBean that Blackie's dad had been arrested and that he and his ma would be going back to her family in Providence. MacBean thought to himself how all his burgeoning business plans were dashed in less than a day. Because Blackie was such a tough kid on the outside, it failed to register with MacBean that Blackie's entire life changed in less than a day. The two thirteen-year old business partners said their goodbyes, vowing to keep in touch through letters, which they did at first, but like so many others who'd made such promises, the letters dwindled down to the occasional Christmas card. Neither boy forgot the other, not because of their successful business, but because they each found in the other someone who would listen to their hopes and dreams for their future without sarcasm or ribbing, but in earnestness. At the time Blackie left, he had wanted to be a car salesman and have a son he could spend time with. MacBean wanted to have a successful business and to give his mum and dad all they deserved.

That knack for business at an early age gave MacBean the confidence to go out in that jungle and make the proverbial buck. It was probably the only time in his life that he could keep a buck in his pocket for any length of time. He was making more money at the deli and kept the newspaper delivery business by subcontracting with younger kids to make the easier deliveries for less pay. He made sure that he got to know the most prominent stock brokers at the deli, most of them working on Wall Street. He knew that by listening to these brokers he could make money in the market. The crash from the Depression was now more than twenty years in the past and World War II was in the recent past, although there was a nasty little war in Korea. Yet business was booming in the United States. He had begun putting his hard-earned money in the market at twelve years old through an account Lonnie had established with Bloomberg's help. MacBean was grateful that he hadn't had a normal childhood because the best times he had were spent conversing with either his parents or the stockbrokers at the deli. Soon enough he had recognized that what he wanted more than anything was to someday be the best-known stockbroker on Wall Street, that center of the investment universe. The brokers that frequented Bloomberg's Deli often left a Wall St. Journal or other investment journals behind them, so he often took them home to study which stocks paid steady dividends. He researched the companies that increased their dividend payout yearly. He invested only in the companies with strong histories and solid plans for their futures. By doing this, he gained a lot of practical knowledge and insight about the market. He would then converse with the brokers at the deli about the stocks he had researched, and they always gave him their opinion on the respective stock. Then he would go home and purchase a few shares of that stock in his dad's name via Mr. Bloomberg's broker. Wise investments would always make a limited income grow.

Historians estimate that between 1949 and 1961, the bull market earned over a 400 percent increase. [(5)]

The U.S. economy was starting to strengthen again after the Depression and war, and that strength lasted throughout MacBean's childhood. Wall Street was just beginning its most successful bull market in U.S. history. The country was in a state of rebuilding, and manufacturing was growing rapidly. MacBean, like any young man in a hurry, wanted no meager wages sitting in a bank earning nothing. He knew in order to grow, money needed to be invested in the stock market with companies like Johnson & Johnson, General Motors, Esso, Procter & Gamble, Coca Cola, DuPont, Merck, Abbott Labs, Texaco, Sears, and Schlumberger. Most of those paid dividends and yet grew in value at the same time. "A double whammy!" MacBean would exclaim at the deli reading the WSJ someone had left there. Those types of companies meant diversification, with pharmaceuticals, gas exploration, soft drinks, chemicals, research, and retail, a nice mix of short-term payoffs and long-term prospects. Of course, MacBean could only purchase one to five shares of each company at first, but to him, it was just the start of great things to come. Later, when he was asked if he had any idea then that he'd see his dream of becoming the best of the best on Wall Street come true, he always responded with a self-effacing, "Of course not". Yet, he'd always believed that if he worked hard enough, anything could happen, just as his parents had taught him.

On the day President Kennedy was assassinated, the Dow fell approximately 3%, but prices recovered within a week, confining the effects primarily to November 22, itself [(6)]

But the innocence, or naivete some would say, of an entire nation was destroyed on November 22, 1963. MacBean was in his trigonometry class when the loud speaker came on with the news. School was dismissed but MacBean decided to go to Bloomberg's before heading home. He made the miscalculation that Bloomberg would be more upset than his parents. The man had a picture of the President hanging in the deli. And when MacBean arrived there, the deli owner was, indeed, upset. And, yet, it was also clear that this was a man who felt at home with tragedy, invited it in, sat it down, and asked it to stay for supper. "It's a sad day, *jungerman*, for us all. That man was such a mensch. Do you know what a mensch is?"

"No" MacBean whispered. It felt as though he should be whispering as Bloomberg was hanging black crepe around the picture.

"A mensch is a real human being".

"Aren't we all human beings?"

"No, I mean someone who understands humanity in all its faults, yet still loves it, is always ready to help. Somebody who is compassionate for all, yet also recognizes that people can cause misery. Even that some people are evil, yet were made that way, not born."

"Then I think you're a mensch, too, Mr. Bloomberg."

"Ahh, that is the best compliment I have ever received."

"Do you think maybe someday I might be a mensch?"

"If you open your eyes, open your heart, and forgive even if not forgetting."

"Do you forgive what happened in World War Two?"

"You ask a question that Jews ask themselves every day. Can you be a mensch if you have not forgiven."

"I could never forgive that: how could anyone?"

"Most of us cannot. But we wish we could. "

"I don't care, you're still a mensch. And I'm just glad I don't have to ever forgive something like that."

"Oh, but there will be many other times when you will ask yourself what to do."

"I know right from wrong. Isn't that enough?"

"Spoken like the true innocent. You have to learn that your right is not always the other person's right. A mensch will look at something from the human angle. Above all, the mensch loves people, not because they are not flawed, but in spite of that. The mensch also knows that he is just as flawed. Life is about learning to love, about embracing one's own humanity, not much else is important."

That last sentence caught MacBean by surprise. *Here was a man who worked most of his life making a success of his deli. How could he possibly mean that wasn't important?*

When MacBean finally arrived home, he realized his miscalculation. Bloomberg was sad for the nation, but his parents were genuinely sad for the death of a young Catholic family man. His mum was openly crying while watching television. His dad walked around with as dour a face as MacBean had ever seen. MacBean was sad, but he couldn't help but wonder what effect this would have on the markets.

MacBean's college boards in the Fall of 1963 were exceptionally high, with a perfect score in math. Many colleges tried to recruit him, but he chose Harvard because, at the time, he thought it would translate into the pinnacle of business success. Harvard was impressed with his abilities to understand the economic environment and the stock market, especially since it was all self-taught. MacBean explained to them that the stocks were held in his dad's name but paid for with MacBean's own money. Harvard accepted him with both a large scholarship established for the promising sons of immigrants and a work study grant. He also learned from a regular deli customer, who specialized in tax matters, that if he filed his own tax return as an independent person when he turned eighteen, his parents could end up having to pay less for his education. His parents were proud of JoJo, as not many kids in 1964 made it to Harvard coming through the public-school system. MacBean knew he would miss his parents terribly; they were his bona fide best friends. But his confidence convinced him that he'd make new friends and that Harvard was the right school, the only school, for JoJo MacBean's future.

If ye like the nut, crack it – Old Scots proverb [7]

When he arrived at Harvard, MacBean was still just seventeen. It was the first time in his life that he had traveled outside of New York City. He also knew it would be a challenge competing with students that had attended private schools all their lives. He was too naïve at that point to have any fear. Most of the other students lived away from home while they attended private schools, so they'd already adjusted to that. Only the thought of his parent's constant love kept him going early on. Most of the Harvard students came from wealthy families, and some of their dads and granddads also graduated from Harvard (or other Ivy League colleges). Money was no object for most of these young men. MacBean was the poor kid on the block, which only served to make him work that much harder.

The thought of being accepted by other students in his age bracket and being together with some of the brightest minds on campus, including world renowned professors, kept him fueled. In a far corner, in the back of his mind, MacBean also imagined himself gaining the courage to communicate with girls at neighboring colleges.

Within the first six weeks of starting school, he was dating most weekends, still allowing plenty of time for studying. One of his new college friends, Jonathan Malone, had arranged a double date. Jonathan's girlfriend, Susan, brought her girlfriend for MacBean's date, which consisted of a movie and a milkshake. He dated Sarah three more times in the next couple weeks, and then she invited him to her room. Both lost their virginity that night, and MacBean believed himself now to be a man. MacBean became a man with four more girls in his freshman year, a fact he chalked up to making up for lost time. He was hoping to find a regular girlfriend, so he could stop wasting time on the pursuit, but as it turned out, no such luck. Still, his freshman year certainly helped his confidence with the girls, least in all the ways that mattered to him at that point. But, at the tail end of that year, he met Rivers Fitzpatrick.

MacBean had no words to explain Rivers. He had fallen deeply in love with her, or so he thought, and had spent three glorious spring months with her while her father was conducting business in Boston for a large bank. Rivers Fitzpatrick was the most beautiful woman MacBean had ever seen. A Radcliffe colleen and daughter of an Irish banker, with her dark wavy hair and eyes so black, the kind one could lose his soul in, and skin the color and smoothness of cream, she was everything he'd never imagined he wanted: romantic, loving, sexy as hell, and with a mind sharper than any he had imagined a young girl would have, and an even sharper tongue. She was also, unlike him, a virgin, which he discovered on their fourth date. He had asked her to marry him. It was testament to her kindness that she didn't laugh at him. She, too, loved him but had no illusions about marrying someone while both of them were still in college. The relationship seemed to be going fine until Rivers asked him what he thought about the Vietnam war.

"Do you not think the U.S. should just give it up?"

"I agree with that. But not for the reasons you've just said. I don't really care about Vietnam; I just don't want our country's resources spent on a war so many experts say can't be won. "

"And when you say 'our country's resources', are you including all the young men who'll be killed or maimed? You weren't talking just about money, were you?"

"I don't want to lie to someone I love. I was talking about financial resources, but you're absolutely right about the men."

"You might want to think about lying to me next time. If there is a next time."

"I just wanted to be honest is all. And I'm glad you brought up the men; you're right of course."

"But you didn't mean them when you first said it. I can't believe I love a man who didn't think of all those young men first!"

"Rivers…"

At that, Rivers stormed out of the dorm room. As she slammed the door she yelled, "Go fuck yourself, Mr. JoJo MacBean."

It would be the first time, but not the last, that he would swear off love. It would be the first, but not the last, time he would tell himself that love was a complication that could only hold him back from success.

With the small amount of money he had, MacBean continued trading stocks listed on the New York Stock Exchange. But, boy, did he miss the conversations with the stockbrokers back at the deli. He was coming to realize that, in the short time he'd been at Harvard, not a day went by that he didn't miss all the Wall Street action.

When sophomore year classes began again in September, it was becoming harder for him to excel due to the level of competition. But he continued to believe that if someone wanted something badly enough, it was achievable. That desire, along with his work ethic, kept him near the top of this class. But his desire was becoming so strong it was transitioning into boredom with classes and impatience with Harvard. He'd begun to think he was wasting valuable time on getting a degree. Here he'd managed to build his personal confidence, make new friends, and be recognized as an equal to his wealthy classmates in terms of future potential. Yet, several times a day, he was thinking about Wall Street, and how soon could he get there. If I can succeed through hard work and desire at Harvard, why can't I do the same on Wall Street? Now!

MacBean had also made some good connections. He knew the importance of such ties, and they kept him from dropping out of Harvard sooner than he did. He had inherited the gift of common sense from his practical Scottish parents. But his plans never included a personal side of life or understanding that a career is not who you are, only what you do. That would come later, much, much later. It all began with Samuel Slade.

"It's not what you know that counts so much as who you know" was first seen in print in 1914 in The Electrical Worker. [8]

MacBean's classmates at Harvard came from a variety of backgrounds. Jonathan Malone's mother was a well-known actress. Some of his other friends' parents were known on a national level: college professors, high-profile lawyers, well known physicians, politicians, owners of sports teams, famous authors, rulers of countries, or Fortune 500 executives. He might have come from the lower end of a middle-class family, but he still felt accepted at Harvard. Maybe it was the clothes his mum tailored for him giving him that confidence. Whatever the case, MacBean had managed to make some friends in college, one of them being Jack Slade. Jack's dad was CEO of Slade Enterprises, Inc., a large company listed on the New York Stock Exchange. Jack's dad would come to the Harvard campus in the autumn to attend one or two Harvard football games. Jack invited MacBean to join them at these games. After the game, Mr. Slade would take both young men to dinner. MacBean was intrigued by Samuel M. Slade, a man with an aura of confidence that he both admired and envied.

Slade Enterprises Inc. was not only listed on the Fortune 500 but it was one of the fifty largest companies on the exchange. MacBean also noted that the elder Slade was always well-dressed, wearing the finest suits he'd ever seen, with impeccable tailoring. MacBean knew his mum's tailoring was as good as any to be had at Louis in Boston or Brooks Brothers in NYC, but Mr. Slade had more than the one best suit MacBean had. He knew one suit alone must have cost the man at least fifteen hundred dollars, and he wore a different one every time MacBean saw him. To say that Samuel M. Slade and MacBean hit it off right away was an understatement. The older Slade clearly took a liking to him, just as the younger one had. Putting his hand on MacBean's shoulder, he often gave him sound advice. To MacBean, Mr. Slade represented everything he wanted to be, from the impeccable manners to the strong, confident personality, from tremendous communication skills to an ability to make quick decisions. MacBean treasured the times the father came to visit his son. He felt that talking with Sam Slade was a lot more interesting than those boring Harvard classes he was taking.

That started MacBean dreaming what it would be like as a Wall Street stockbroker and Mr. Slade his own client. Somewhere deep within MacBean's heart, he knew that someday, somehow, that dream would become reality. MacBean also knew that this was a contact that could help him achieve that dream. Such contacts were all important. Without them, he'd be just another faceless broker like the ones at the deli. Nice guys, making better than decent livings, but not in the stratosphere that MacBean was aiming for.

When the time was right, he would ask his friend, Jack, questions about his dad. Jack always told him his daddy never spent much time with him due to the long hours of work plus his traveling on business trips all over the world. Jack also said that his mom never spent much time with him either, since Mrs. Slade often accompanied her husband on many of his business trips. On top of this, Jack said that he went to a lot of summer camps during his school years and that the times he had with his dad were precious but few, most often the occasional Saturday or Sunday afternoon. Jack told me that going to dinner with his dad after a game was about the only quality time he got to spend with him. "Sure, once in a while we had vacations". he said, "but it was never enough for me because I'd just end up missing him again once we returned home."

Slade Enterprises had plants in the United States and all over the world. The enterprise was so vast that he was traveling over fifty percent of the time. Jack had told him that his dad was good about checking in on him by phone wherever he was, always making sure he was doing OK. He said that he knew his dad cared about him, but they weren't long phone calls, somebody was always interrupting him. MacBean, on the other hand, was on the phone with his dad at least three or four times a month. They never talked long either, but that was because of the phone bill, not dad's time! In fact, MacBean had noted that several of the kids that went to private schools before attending Harvard didn't really spend much time with their successful parents. He realized he was truly blessed that he'd had a good amount of time with his wonderful mum and dad. He didn't think the parents didn't love their sons or daughters, it was just that in their world, future success didn't depend on it, so it was relegated to less than top priority. Those young men seemed more resigned than excited about their future life being just like their fathers'. Yet, oddly enough, MacBean did not see the incongruity between wanting the kind of success that Mr. Slade had and feeling badly that Jack had missed out on a close relationship with his parents, such as MacBean had.

As the semester wore on, MacBean became increasingly bored with the classroom. He thought that four or five years of college was about ten percent of his working career and that he was wasting his time instead of making money. Wouldn't it be wiser to spend his time working and earning? The summer after his freshmen year he'd returned home for the summer, having earned close to a 3.5 cumulative average. Mr. Bloomberg was kind enough to take him on for the summer. His heart was raring to start a business career. No longer was he cleaning the floors at the deli. Now he was waiting on customers, with a keen ear for listening to the stock brokers talk about the market as he worked away. He knew every broker that frequented the deli and was learning a lot from them. Mr. Bloomberg thought that learning from his customers was a good experience for him. Some of the brokers gave him encouragement by telling him that if he ever made it to being a broker, he'd have a wonderful career. They all saw his enthusiasm for the stock market, but he needed them to see he had so much more than that.

As he went to dinner after a Saturday football game with Jack and Sam Slade, he could not stop thinking about Mr. Slade's business career. Every time MacBean observed this professionally polished businessman, it only confirmed in him that he was wasting precious time attending Harvard.

It was still a bull market, and the economy had been extremely strong for almost twenty years, with U.S. gross domestic product averaging a robust 7.3 percent and the market averaging 10.3 percent return. MacBean wanted badly to be a part of this, to hop on the gravy train that was Wall Street. It felt like a "now or never" moment in his life. Sounding strange in a twenty-year-old, he'd been dreaming of this since he was ten, mopping floors and reading discarded WSJs at the deli.

Thus, despite his continued 3.5 cumulative the first semester of his sophomore year, JoJo MacBean declared he would withdraw from Harvard at the completion of his sophomore year.

The name Wall Street originated because the 17thc. Dutch settlers of lower Manhattan Island literally built a wall to keep out native Americans, the British, and pirates. Since the Dutch leader had ordered the massacre of native Americans in at least one instance, the wall was a tactical necessity. [(9)]

BROAD ST.
WALL ST.

2

CONQUERING WALL STREET
1966 – 1984

The market began in 1966 at 969 and ended 1984 at 1211. 1966 began a sixteen-year bear market that ended in 1982. (10)

MacBean's parents were dismayed and worried that Cambridge had proven too much for their shy, isolated son, and Sam Slade and Sol Bloomberg were also disappointed. Yet MacBean was determined to get a job on Wall Street, even if he had to work from the ground up. MacBean reasoned that he'd gained some life experience and made enough contacts in two years that might prove valuable. He was a quick student of the "who you know" principle, in fact he'd already seen it demonstrated. And he had no doubt that he had the brain power to stay at Harvard and excel – if he wanted to.

He figured by withdrawing from Harvard he added two years to his full-time business career. However, he knew neither his parents nor any of the other adults in his life would see it that way. To them, the education of a college degree was not just the first priority but a requirement for success of any kind. Yet MacBean knew in his heart that his was to be a different path than his classmates because he was so different from them.

He considered Bloomberg a success without a degree. He considered his dad a success without a degree. He knew there was still a lot to learn, but he also knew in his gut that he could achieve the same level of business success without that degree, as Mr. Slade had. Of course, MacBean's thinking amounted to equating success solely with making money, the kind of thinking that his parents knew was typical of the youthfully naïve. MacBean believed that a desire as strong as his would overcome any and every obstacle in its way.

He had no worries about starting completely at the bottom and working his way to the top of a Wall Street brokerage firm, if he could just get that initial break. Focused and driven, he had no other goal than to get that job.

Back to living at home, and no longer with the panache of being a Harvard student, MacBean was barely twenty and working six-hour days at Bloomberg's Deli, six days a week. He started early in the day to allow himself precious time to pound the pavement on Wall Street looking for any job he could get. The street, itself, was a mixture of the old and the new, of stone and steel, wood and glass, the most prime piece of real estate perhaps in the world. It took him over a week just to fill out job applications for the numerous companies located in a single Wall Street building. Most of the companies there were prestigious brokerage firms and national headquarters for banks and Fortune 500 Companies.

MacBean pounded those Wall Street doors every chance he had, seeking the opportunity to get his business career started. Even though rejected in most places, a few of the companies let him complete their job application. In spite of bouts of frustration, he never lost his iron determination. Every time he went to the brokerage houses and got a glimpse of the stock brokers working at a hectic pace, it refueled his engines, put his mind into overdrive, and made him double down, and double down again, and then again, on his job seeking. He even dreamed about being one of them. He never had a scintilla of doubt that eventually he would succeed.

The stock brokers that came into Bloomberg's Deli were a lot of fun to converse with, but very few of them knew the top echelon of brokers on Wall Street personally, so they would be no help in landing a position there. *I'll need to make my own opportunity, to create my own break. I've done it before, I'll do it again.*

After several weeks of applications, phone calls, and strategizing, MacBean called Jack Slade, who was finishing the first half of his junior year at Harvard. It occurred to him that he should ask Jack if he knew his dad's stockbroker. Jack didn't have the answer to that, but he did tell him that his Dad was traveling that week and would be at the Omni Hotel in Atlanta during his business trip. Jack told MacBean he would call him back with his dad's room and phone number.

When Jack called him the next day, he said his dad would be expecting a call between eight and nine P.M. Samuel Slade worked even later hours on his business trips, socializing with many of his business contacts. Those long hours meant he could get back to the home office a little quicker each trip.

MacBean made perhaps the most important call of his life the next evening. Mr. Slade said that he was sorry to see MacBean leave Harvard because he had been doing so well. He advised MacBean to consider going back there to complete his education. A Harvard degree meant something in the upper echelons of the business world.

"Mr. Slade", MacBean responded, "my number one goal right now is to get any type of position with a Wall Street brokerage firm. Jack told me that your broker was one of the best known on Wall Street, but he, ha ha, couldn't remember his name. I was hoping you could do me a favor and ask your broker if he could obtain an interview for me with his company. I would be glad to meet with your broker first, and if he felt comfortable with me, maybe he could recommend me for any type of position within his company. I know that if I can get a break of any kind, Mr. Slade, that company will not regret it. I also understand that I have to start somewhere and that somewhere's probably close to the bottom."

Mr. Slade responded, "Well, MacBean, first let me correct you. It's not going to be close to the bottom, it would be the bottom. My broker's name is Harvey Bernstein. Harvey works for Kurtzner Brothers, LTD, otherwise known as KBL. KBL is the most prestigious brokerage firm in the world. That is a tall order that you want me to fill. I am sure that I am one of Mr. Bernstein's best clients, but I can assure you that will not carry enough weight to get you in the front door at KBL. I will tell you what I will do, but I must ask on one condition." MacBean asked Mr. Slade what the condition was, and he answered, "You will have to pay me back for that favor. You see, I never asked Mr. Bernstein for a favor in my entire life, and I have known him for many years."

"What favor might that be Mr. Slade?"

"If you get a job with the Kurtzner Brothers, and I mean any type of job, you will pay me back by resuming your college education part-time somewhere and get that business degree. Hopefully you can do that in New York City. There are enough colleges there where you could major in finance. You see, I took a liking to you, and I know that you have the ingredients to succeed. What impressed me the most about you was that you excelled in the Harvard classrooms, and yet you never attended a private school prior to your entrance there. That is not a small feat but quite an accomplishment. You need lots of polish, but you certainly have unlimited potential. I do not say this lightly because I do not see potential very often, especially in kids your age. I know a diamond in the rough when I see one. But you also need to educate yourself not just in finance, but more broadly. It'll help with your communication skills and understanding of others, as well as with seeing there's more than just Wall Street in this wide world". That last sentence shocked MacBean, coming from a man who had clearly made vast amounts of money on Wall Street. But knowing he had such confidence in MacBean made him think if he could be half the person Mr. Slade was, he would be a happy guy. He certainly had given MacBean pause to think about his future.

"Mr. Slade," MacBean said as his heart was pounding like it never did before, "I promise I will look into starting college immediately".

"Never mind looking into it – do it!"

MacBean knew then that he could not let Mr. Slade down. He had become as important to MacBean as his parents were because of his kindness in caring about a young man with big dreams. MacBean thought back to Mr. Bloomberg and realized he was a lucky kid to have two such mentors helping him along.

Mr. Slade ended his part of the conversation with a promise to MacBean that on his next business trip to New York City, he would look the young man up, and they would get together for dinner. MacBean was never so excited in his life, even without a promise yet for an interview. He just had a gut feeling that the tide was turning, and good things were about to come his way. He'd always felt fortunate that Jack had Mr. Slade for his dad. Talk about the right place at the right time. He knew that success was a lot of hard work, but it also mattered who you met along the way and how you treated them because you never knew when or how respect or kindness might be returned.

MacBean spent the next day researching Harvey X. Bernstein. He had an MBA from Wharton School of Business and was one of the premiere traders on Wall Street. He was often quoted in the Wall Street Journal and Barron's; in fact, well over a thousand times, many of them were on the front page. Presidents Truman, Eisenhower, Kennedy, and probably Johnson solicited his advice on the U.S. economy. Harvey was also an occasional guest on television discussing the status of the US economy and other related financial matters.

About four weeks after MacBean talked to Mr. Slade, Harvey Bernstein telephoned. He apologized for taking so long to get back to him. "Working sixteen hours a day, it's sometimes hard to find the time to make calls not directly related to business," Mr. Bernstein stated. MacBean expressed his appreciation to Mr. Bernstein for even remembering to give him a call. Harvey said that Mr. Slade had reminded him a couple times in the last couple weeks to call. "When Mr. Slade talks, I better listen. After all," he said, "Sam is just about my favorite client, and a good friend to boot."

Mr. Slade was indeed the most influential person MacBean had met up to this point in his life. Harvey then asked what he would like to do, to which MacBean replied by telling him that he would take any job with Kurtzner Brothers Limited. He would do anything to get a start in KBL including mopping the floors. Harvey started chuckling and saying, "That would not be necessary. Our company is not even accepting job applications at the moment Also, everyone that works here in any type of decent position has at least a B.A. in business or finance. It would be a tough sell to get you a position with this company, but I will tell you what, I do work through lunch hour because of the large list of clientele I have. I will get my team to handle all my phone calls for a half an hour or so next Tuesday afternoon between 12:30 and 1. I will order us a couple of turkey sandwiches while I have a meeting with you. How's that?"

"Mr. Bernstein, I have worked part-time at a kosher deli for several years, and they make the best Reuben sandwiches in New York City. Do you like Reubens?"

"Only if it has a good kosher pickle and a celery soda to go with it."

"I guess you know something about delis. I will be there at 12:30 sharp, Mr. Bernstein and I'll be bringing the lunch".

The first thing MacBean did after receiving that phone call was to contact his mum to ask for a favor. He needed a three-piece suit, the finest suit she'd ever tailored, and by next Monday. Claire responded that she would do this if she could pick out a tie and a new pair of shoes to go with it, since her taste was much better than her son's. Claire also promised to have the suit ready for a fitting by Sunday, so he could try it on, and then she could make her final adjustments on Monday morning. MacBean's mum wasn't just a perfectionist at what she did, she knew that her tailoring represented Claire MacDyer to the world. She was just as excited as he was, getting very little sleep the next few days. MacBean didn't sleep very well either because he recognized how important his upcoming meeting with Mr. Bernstein was to his future. Over and over in his mind, he kept trying to figure out what he should talk about with Mr. Bernstein for a half hour. *I could tell him that I'd been investing in the market through an account under my dad's name since I was ten years old. It was proof I had a knack for making a profit even on small investments. Almost every purchase of stock that I'd ever bought was up over its initial purchase price. But so were stocks I'd never purchased. How do I answer that?* MacBean also realized that his lack of education could hinder the possibility of obtaining a position at Kurtzner Brothers. *Did Mr. Slade have it right after all? Had I made the biggest mistake of my life by age twenty?*

What else could I talk about with Mr. Bernstein? Should I tell him that I would listen to the broker's converse about the market during my working hours at the deli, and those were, by far, the most interesting hours of my day; that the brokers provided me at a young age with an insight into what I wanted to become. Or that I started studying up on the market very early on, and I actually was current on the hot stocks in the market that an investor could make money on..? How much was too much? How much was enough?

MacBean knew that his approach was to think long-term regarding investments because people work hard for their money, and every investor has different outlooks, different long-term goals. He also knew that he could make more money in a half hour of trading stocks than he could in a whole month working at the deli, if he just had a chance. While other kids were buying baseball cards, bicycles, and movie tickets,

MacBean was giving his dad his meager savings to put into the market. MacBean ultimately knew his only hope was that Mr. Bernstein would take a personal interest in him because of MacBean's background. *How many other eleven-year-old kids knew how to buy and sell stocks? How many knew to start buying shares in utility stocks and the old staples like GM and Ford Motors and the Ma Bell group of companies? I invested in companies that provided consumer products and services that I thought would be around for a hundred plus years. With a strong economy in the fifties and into the early sixties, I was making good sound and safe decisions. Would Bernstein find me interesting enough?* MacBean also realized that Mr. Slade had probably already told Mr. Bernstein everything about me he would need to know. Slade always knew the right things to say, he'd built his success on that skill. Eventually MacBean screamed to himself, *Enough, just be myself, for better or worse. It's the most important half hour of my life so far, but if I can't be myself, it won't amount to much anyway!*

That Sunday night, MacBean dreamed he'd become one of Bernstein's assistants and had worked himself up to his number one man. But it was only a dream. He tried on the beautiful dark blue three-piece pinstriped suit that his mum tailored for him. She had even tailored a custom-made white shirt and bought gold plated cufflinks and a tie to go along with a beautiful pair of black dress shoes. MacBean knew his poor mum must have spent a fortune on him for this upcoming interview. Between nerves and happiness, he and his mum both broke down and cried as he looked into the mirror at the expensively dressed business man staring back. "I'll pay you back, Mum, I will." But the payment she wanted back was only to keep his promise to Mr. Slade and finish his college education. That very Monday morning, early in June, MacBean registered at the College of Manhattan, choosing two summer courses of basic accounting and finance 101. He was hopeful that adrenaline would prevail over his lack of sleep. He made a point of reminding himself to be an attentive listener when the businessman spoke.

MacBean's interview was set for Tuesday at 12:30 P.M. As he dressed, his mum said he looked better than a million dollars. He went to the deli about 11:30 A.M. and ordered his two Reuben sandwiches, two celery sodas, and two kosher pickles. Mr. Bloomberg stood for a minute and just stared at him. Then he took hold of MacBean's hand in a mighty handshake saying, "Now go out there and make me proud!"

He arrived at Bernstein's office twenty minutes early. At precisely 12:30 P.M., Mr. Bernstein told his secretary to bring MacBean into his office.

Mr. Bernstein enjoyed the delicious lunch. 'What a Reuben!' he stated. After all, MacBean's worries, he hadn't even said that much. Mr. Bernstein looked at him at the end of the half hour interview and said, "I'm sorry, Mr. MacBean, but all I can offer you is a job as a stock boy for three hundred a week. You'd be working about fifty hours a week." MacBean replied that he'd meant it when he said he'd start anywhere and was very grateful to get this opportunity. He wasn't really expecting to be hired at this interview, so Mr. Bernstein took him by surprise. But oh, what a pleasant surprise. MacBean didn't care if he started off at KBL as a janitor. He now had a career path! A very long one, but still a path.

"OK, then, JoJo, go to the Personnel Department two floors down, and complete your job application. Be here at 6 A.M. next Monday morning to meet with Stanley Smith. Mr. Smith is in charge of the stockroom, which consists of ten employees, including you".

MacBean thanked Mr. Bernstein, to which he replied that he should be thanking Mr. Slade, not him. The CEO of Kurtzner Brothers LTD, Joshua Ornsby, valued Mr. Slade as a client, so MacBean owed all of this to Mr. Slade. "I'll be here by 5:45 A.M. sir," he responded. "And I hope to see you."

Mr. Bernstein replied, "Oh, we will run into each other now and then. Oh, by the way, Jack Slade said everybody calls you

MacBean. Which do you prefer, JoJo or MacBean?"

"Mr. Bernstein, you can call me anything you want! But MacBean is what my friends call me, and with what you're doing for me today, I'd have to say you're a friend now."

If you cannot do great things, do small things in a great way – Napoleon Hill [11]

Maybe it was just paper shuffling, but MacBean still felt he had arrived on Wall Street. He felt invincible, as though nothing could stop him now as he climbed the proverbial ladder from the bottom right up to the very top. Focused on succeeding in this company MacBean put the rest of his personal life, outside of his college courses, on hold. He was planning on being at the ladder's top of Kurtzner Brothers LTD, sooner rather than later.

Three hundred dollars a week for a fifty-hour work week wasn't much in 1966, but living at home helped. He knew he'd need to prove what he was capable of. He also knew he could work a few extra hours at the deli if he needed to supplement his income, particularly for making investments of his own.

That Monday, MacBean showed up at 5:15 A.M., earlier than even the 5:45 he'd promised, for his first day of work as a stock boy for the most prestigious brokerage firm on Wall Street. He also started his three courses the same week at the College of Manhattan. It certainly wasn't Harvard, but the promise to Mr. Slade was important to keep. The courses he took were not that challenging, so he still felt he had plenty of energy to give to KBL.

As the low guy on the totem pole, he knew he had to earn his way up that ladder. He made sure that all brokers at all times were kept supplied with the proper paperwork to service their clients in order to make trades. He learned about all the security forms quickly and even studied them in detail by bringing them home. No broker ever had to call if they were running low on forms, as he tracked their usage and stayed on top of the situation constantly. He was sure the brokers would notice that no one ever ran out of forms under his watch. He knew he had to take this job seriously if he wanted anyone else to take him seriously.

"Next time, buy more pepperoni, less cheese" someone shouted from the back.

"You got it, man". Even the pizza he brought to the brokers was always correct, MacBean having figured out that giving the pizza place a tip ensured accuracy. Since the brokers usually tipped him, he figured it was worth the few bucks to earn the reputation as someone they could rely on – every time, even for something as unimportant as pizza. But what MacBean did with his discovery shot him into the stratosphere of clerks – he told all the other clerks, so they would always get pizzas right, too. He hadn't told them to be generous, he was just having to get up to twenty pizzas a day because no one wanted anyone but MacBean to get them. Expediency made him share his secret, but doing that sharing made everyone think that MacBean was a real team player. And in a highly competitive business, being a team player demonstrated an incredible amount of self-confidence and commitment first, and foremost, to the company.

It was hot in back of that stock room that first summer of his new career. It seemed like he was taking inventory constantly on the forms that the brokers used, making sure they always had a good supply of all the forms. The pace was hectic; ten hours a day, each and every day. But the time went by quickly. It was a nice break when he got to deliver the forms to the air-conditioned trading floor. There, he would observe the brokers trading at a hectic pace. He had a few glimpses of Bernstein and the other brokers, but they seldom noticed him. They simply were too busy, working at a furious pace, high on all the coffee they drank, as well as the stress and excitement of the floor. He put in extra time almost every day except for class nights. Soon, MacBean knew he was being noticed for his dedication to a lowly stockroom job!

His motivation to succeed was the key to laying down a foundation to secure a successful career as a broker. He was working for the cream of the crop of brokerage firms, and he looked for every opportunity to observe each broker and to understand that broker's individual needs, not just for forms but for information.

It was now mid-1967, MacBean was twenty years old, and it was a literally the crack of dawn of the computer age. Computers were still large, very pricey and only the top companies could afford them, with all the data entry done mostly by women. The entry work took two work shifts a day because initially, the computers were very slow. But MacBean knew a potential mega-trend when he saw one, and he began registering for as many computer classes at Manhattan College as he could fit into his busy schedule.

The brokers at KBL were all making over a million dollars a year. Compared to MacBean's three hundred a week, it was a salary he could only dream about. The brokers on Wall Street made much more than a baseball superstar. Only a handful of ball players were breaking a hundred thousand a year, including the toast of New York, Mickey Mantle.

As the weeks went by, he became acquainted with several other brokers at KBL. There was Jacob Kahn, a slick-looking, neatly dressed man with a head of shiny black hair, complements of Brill Cream, that was always groomed perfectly. MacBean had heard that his suits cost well over two thousand each. His tailors measured him up right at the office before he started working at 6:30 A.M.

There was also Salvatore Fusaro. Sal had a strong Italian accent, and he could speak several languages. This gained him many international clients. Mr. Fusaro had an A-1 personality. He would occasionally ask MacBean if he could pick him up some lunch, and he would give him a ten-dollar tip. Of course, he'd pop over to Bloomberg's. Money was no object for the brokers at KBL. These brokers would never leave their desks during lunch hours because some of the most important phone calls from all over the world would come in at that time. That is one of the reasons why the best brokers were high strung. They never stopped the hectic pace once their long work day began.

Mr. Harold Hoffberg was an old, bald gentleman, in his mid-seventies, who had been a broker for nearly forty-seven years, starting just after WWI. He was the exception that proved the rule, coming into work usually around eleven and leaving promptly at three. He had assembled quite a staff to assist him with his clientele. MacBean enjoyed listening to him talk about the '29 crash, and how he had actually seen a man jump out a window. He also told MacBean about the Lindbergh ticker tape parade, with real ticker tape. The old broker's stories about John D. Rockefeller and Andrew Carnegie made MacBean realize that Wall Street wasn't a mere geographical location, but a state of mind. A very greedy state of mind in many cases, but also the state of mind that created the wealth necessary to create the infrastructure of this country. Next to Bloomberg, MacBean loved listening to Harold reminisce.

All of the brokers at KBL had customer lists, and these brokers and their assistants took care of customer needs. KBL provided services to their clientele as close to perfect as one could imagine.

In autumn, he picked up two more college courses-Economics, Statistics and another computer course. He figured that his work environment would help a great deal with these courses, and he was right. That, in turn, allowed MacBean to devote more time to his job. MacBean still worked an occasional Sunday at the deli when his old boss needed him.

After a few months at KBL most of the brokers sensed that the young Scotsman had the desire to someday be one of them. He was clearly "growing" on them in the most positive way.

Many of the brokers had begun – finally - talking to him about the market. And he knew this was one way to show them his skills in the world of trading. The brokers at KBL were now aware that he had a keen eye for the market and that he paid close and detailed attention to all the companies listed on the exchange.

Setting an example is not the main means of influencing others; it is the only means.
Albert Einstein [(12)]

THREE WISE MEN

On occasion, the brokers had small confrontations with each other about certain business issues, and MacBean astutely observed that such differences were handled not only professionally, but gracefully. He could see why KBL was considered at the top of the heap. The bottom line was always to pay attention to each of the individual client needs. Some of the brokers were even beginning to ask MacBean his opinion on certain stocks, and, usually, he gave them a prompt answer. Sometimes it required a little lunch time research. And he was always cautious when they asked him for an opinion. He couldn't give wrong answers and keep them asking; thus, the research was important. But his growing knowledge about the market impressed most of the brokers, and eventually he was being asked on a daily basis about certain stocks. Along with hard work and obtaining knowledge on what would become his field of expertise, he was acquiring the ingredients for a successful career.

Harold Hoffberg said to MacBean one day, "You'd better start studying for the security exams because you are going to end up being a broker somewhere in the near future." MacBean whispered to the old broker that he had already passed most of the security exams. "Why does that not surprise me?" the old man stated. Hoffberg smiled and then shook MacBean's hand while MacBean told him that he had started studying for these exams the day he started working at KBL and that he had passed all the courses he'd studied for. Mr. Hoffberg was impressed that MacBean had accomplished so much in such a short time. "It's remarkable to find such a clear vision in a young man these days," Hoffberg said. "I can see you going a long way in this line of business, young man. Keep up the good work."

MacBean was now learning to read financial statements of the larger companies and the up and coming companies that were listed on the exchange. All these companies hired independent certified public accountants to prepare financial statements for the stockholders of the entities. Of course, the banks and the stockbrokers relied on this financial information, also. These statements were available to the general public if someone wanted to research them to see if there were any kinds of investment opportunities available in any of their enterprises. Most of the accounting services for the companies listed on the exchange were prepared by the "Big Eight" accounting firms, the most elite group in the field: Price Waterhouse, Arthur Anderson, Touche Ross, Arthur Young, Peat Marwick Mitchell, and others of lesser household name status. All of these companies were international CPA firms with offices not only located around the U.S. but in many other countries. Two weeks later, Harvey Bernstein asked MacBean if he would have dinner with him at 9 P.M. Bernstein knew he had a college course, and he said that they could meet at Rein's Deli after his class.

When MacBean met Bernstein at the deli, he got right to the point. "Harold Hoffberg informed me that you passed most of the security exams, is that true?"

"Yes sir" he replied.

"Why didn't you tell me about this?" Bernstein responded.

"Well sir, I knew that I had to start somewhere with the company, and I was hoping that someday I could work myself up the ladder in KBL. I thought that I should try to pass those exams on my own, so that I could be prepared for this when the opportunity arose. At this point in my early career, I know there is still a lot to learn. You, and Mr. Slade, of course, provided me with the opportunity to be a part of KBL. I just wanted to prepare in advance for my future… that is all I wanted to do, sir. I didn't think that my passing these exams would concern anyone at that point in time. "

Bernstein continued, "Some of the brokers at KBL like your willingness to do a little research at lunch hour when called upon, and they feel that you have a strong knack for this type of work. I am one of those who is starting to believe in you. I am beginning to see what my dear friend, Sam Slade, was talking about. Oh, by the way, Sam should be here at about nine-thirty. He's in town on business."

"Wow," MacBean replied," it will be nice to see Mr. Slade again"

"He is here for a few days," Bernstein stated. "In fact, I am spending Saturday and Sunday with Sam on his yacht. We are flying to Miami, where his yacht is docked, on Friday night. There is much business to discuss over the weekend, so we can combine business with a little pleasure".

"Great!" MacBean replied, hoping someday he would be in the same position as Sam Slade. At just that moment, Samuel Slade walked into Reins Deli and gave MacBean a firm handshake and a huge hug.

"So good to see you, Mr. Slade," MacBean said.

"Call me Sam now, son," It was hard for MacBean to keep his emotions in check.

Sam asked right away, "MacBean, what are you doing about the college situation?"

"Well sir, I've taken four business and finance courses thus far at College of Manhattan as you suggested. I am currently taking two more courses, and I added in a couple computer courses, too."

Slade grinned and said, "Well done, and keep it up." He knew that MacBean had made a promise he would not dare to disregard.

While still at the dinner table, it was Bernstein's turn to talk to MacBean. "I wanted Sam here tonight. Not only is Sam a client, he is a good friend, and I wanted Sam to share this moment with us. Sam was correct when he said to me that he thought you would have a promising future. Of course, I have always valued Sam's opinions. I want you to become one of my research assistants to help me service my demanding clientele. I already informed Sam that you passed most of the security exams already. Have you been fingerprinted?" MacBean nodded yes. Bernstein went on, "My assistants research stocks that my investors could make money on in the long term. As you know, long-term capital gains provide a tax break on the income gained. This means a lot for our high bracket clientele. Many of my clients also look for solid dividend paying stocks. As you know, minimizing risk is of the upmost importance at KBL. Although you will be at the bottom of the ladder, again, in this new department, you will be a research assistant. It is a very important step for your future in this business. You're a brilliant young man with a knack for the market, but don't let that go to your head. Your pay will be raised to five hundred a week". Bernstein finished with a big smile, but no bigger than MacBean's.

Sam Slade then said to him, "Keep in mind that five hundred a week in New York City is like making half that in most parts of the country"

"I am aware of that sir. That's why I still live at home with my parents, so I can save what I make".

"Do you mind if I ask you how much you've saved?"

"I have about nine thousand of my own savings invested in the market, and today it is worth slightly more than thirty thousand," he replied as modestly as he could. Mr. Bernstein then asked MacBean how old he was. MacBean replied, "I just turned twenty-one last Christmas".

"That's fine, fine. Even though the minimum brokerage account at KBL is a million, you can transfer your thirty thousand to open an KBL account in your name, since you work for us. Of course, you will be in charge of your own account. But you will not be permitted to borrow on margin".

"Don't worry sir, with my new salary and living at home, I should be able to add six hundred a month to my investment account. I really appreciate this opportunity, Mr. Bernstein! I thought it would take a little more time to work my way up through the stockroom first, so thank you for your confidence in me sir."

Bernstein replied, "A matter of economics, MacBean. You've proven yourself too valuable to us to waste more time shuffling forms."

MacBean then turned to Sam Slade and said, "It's all because of you, Sam, and of course Mr. Bernstein. It's so good to see you again", said MacBean, as he shook Slade's hand.

Slade replied, "It was good to see you, too, son, and please stay in touch with Jack: he misses you. He's also talking some nonsense about enlisting, got it in his head it's what I would do. I enlisted in WW2, every able-bodied single guy did, many married guys, too, since it was likely they'd be drafted anyway. Hell yes, I'd be proud of him if he enlisted, our country's in a war, even if nobody's declared it. I'm from a generation that believes when your country calls, you answer. But I don't want to lose my son, MacBean. Kids are dying over there. Maybe you can talk some sense into him." As he left, Sam Slade looked back at him, smiled, and gave him a wink. MacBean had seen him do that to Jack, and it made him feel as though he'd been officially adopted into the Slade family. First, Mr. Bloomberg, then Sam Slade, and now Harvey Bernstein. After his own parents, the three people whose confidence made MacBean proud enough to know he would never disappoint any of them. These three were instrumental in laying down the foundation for his future. MacBean began to think of them as his personal three wise men, bringing not presents but belief in him. He wondered whether their expectations might not be more than he could meet, but his visions of Wall Street success always managed to push such thoughts out of his mind. He was also grateful for the tendency to severe motion sickness as a child that he hoped would earn him a 4-F, if that dreaded notice ever arrived in his mailbox.

Dow Chemical, the company that produced the napalm used in the Vietnam War, was often the target of protestors during the war years.. Yet on college campuses during that time, the number of students interviewing for potential jobs with Dow increased, proving that even bad publicity creates positive visibility for a company. (13)

UP THE WALL STREET LADDER

All the brokers at KBL had high profile clients. Like many other highly experienced brokers for more than twenty years, Mr. Bernstein's clients had to have a minimum balance of two and a half million dollars in their respective accounts. In MacBean's short time as one of Bernstein's research assistants, he realized that a multitude of the clients had accounts exceeding ten million dollars. Bernstein also had several clients with assets of over one hundred million. Bernstein's clients included former U.S. presidents, governors, congressman, senators, and world leaders, including a sheik, two kings, a queen, and at least a hundred CEOs of Fortune 500 companies and other large companies, both publicly and privately held. MacBean had met some of the athletes, authors, and entertainers that had also achieved the status of being a Bernstein client. Unlike most of the clients, those were the kinds that didn't mind talking with researchers about their wealth; it was part of how they earned it. Mr. Bernstein's client list was a who's who of movers and shakers, and Bernstein, himself, was the cream of the crop when it came down to who's who in the brokerage industry.

Within four months of MacBean starting his research job and beginning to make recommendations for a variety of Harvey Bernstein's clients, MacBean became the top researcher on his research team. Bernstein originally had eight employees on this staff, but once MacBean took the lead, Bernstein let two researchers go and immediately raised MacBean's salary to eight-hundred a week. Even with the raise, Bernstein saved money by cutting labor costs because MacBean's fierce work ethic translated into getting things done more quickly. It was a win-win situation for both MacBean and Bernstein. MacBean remembered saying "goodbye" to the two fellows let-go as he thought *that's the biz*.

When someone asked him a few days later if he knew what the two men had for plans of employment, MacBean replied, "Honestly, I don't know". *It's not my job to know. My job is to make money for KBL, and that I'm doing in spades!* Many of the positive results came from his predictions of where the market was going, and where it was trending. Some thought it was uncanny, but it was just old-fashioned dogged research, including keeping his ears to the ground for rumors that he could then verify. It was clear to everyone that rumors were important bits of information, information that could lead to future profits. But the line between listening to a rumor and trading on insider information was a thin one. MacBean became not just a master of walking that line, but of finding ways to move the line to his advantage when necessary.

The stock market is not one giant entity, but made up of a multitude of sectors including manufacturing, computers and related technology, the health industry including the pharmaceutical sector, which is ten times larger than most people realize, retail and wholesale, the financial sector including banks and insurance companies, and a few emerging companies that depended on venture capital, such as startups in the solar industry, a craze at that time. His clients had never been so satisfied as when he began working at KBL. His first Christmas, Bernstein presented him with a ten-thousand-dollar bonus, which he wasn't expecting. He bought his parents a round trip air flight to Scotland plus car rental and walking around cash for a two week visit with their families. It was their first trip back to Scotland since they arrived in the United States forty years before. The tears of joy in his parents' eyes was a moment he would always cherish. Of course, after they said "thank you", they brought up that they hoped his success didn't mean he wouldn't finish college. MacBean told them that he was now more than half way to his B.A. because Manhattan College had finally accepted his Harvard credits. The rest of the bonus was invested, putting him on pace to make sixty thousand in his first full year at KBL. He never remembered being happier than that Christmas of 1968, when he turned twenty-two.

WALL STREET - MACBEAN STREET

By March of '69, MacBean's salary was a thousand a week. *Thank God I hadn't wasted more time at Harvard.* He made the decision that it was now the right time to move out of his parents' home. It wasn't that he particularly wanted to, he felt it was what someone was supposed to do. Although, his Scottish upbringing was also telling him he'd be giving up money that could be otherwise invested. It was his mother that finally convinced him by telling him that a young woman would never want to marry a man who was still living with his parents. And though he might not be looking for a wife, she was most definitely looking for some grandchildren. "Now skedaddle" she said.

Thanks to Mr. Bernstein, MacBean found a tiny Manhattan "closet" for twelve-hundred a month. With his recent raise, he budgeted eleven hundred a month for savings but found himself surprised at how much utilities cost. He began to wonder how Bloomberg made any money at the deli after paying utilities, especially with a large, cold meat locker and all those refrigerated deli cases. He left home telling his parents he would call them every day, even if it was only for one minute, and he'd stop for supper at least once a week. Some days he worked late, so his mum would heat up his meal when he'd call from work to tell her he was just then leaving the office. But most weeks MacBean had to wait until Sunday to have that weekly meal. Even then it became sporadic.

Claire continued to make his suits, always picking out the accessories as well. And like many mums, she was only too happy to do his weekly laundry. Also, like many a mother and son, neither Claire nor MacBean saw spoiling her son as detrimental to his future relationships.

MacBean slept in his cubby hole a few hours a night after working long hours and taking his college courses. A year into the job, he no longer had the time to help occasionally at the deli on a Sunday. He had promised Mr. Bloomberg that he would visit him at the deli which he managed to do almost every month. Of course, he would eat for free at Sol's insistence. MacBean also, strictly off the record, gave the old deli owner a few stock tips that paid off for him. MacBean knew he could eat there every day, and Mr. Bloomberg would be fine with it, but he didn't want to take advantage of him. Sol Bloomberg had become tantamount to family. MacBean had seen the amount of time Bloomberg spent at his deli, and MacBean knew that kind of dedication was necessary in order to succeed at anything. "Brains are important", the deli owner always said, "but without hard work, they're nothing more than gefilte fish".

MacBean's own portfolio managed to reach fifty thousand within a couple months shy of his latest promotion. He limited the time spent on his personal account to just fifteen minutes a day. He didn't have any more time than that even if he'd wanted it. Bernstein was about fifty-five years old and at the peak of his Wall Street career. But MacBean took note that within a few months after joining his team, the continuous hectic pace of a long work day was starting to take its toll on him. MacBean observed that it was as though Bernstein hit a wall of some kind and from that point started to age quickly. What he did not observe was the older broker's sadness that all his money wasn't going to save him from a life of stress, lack of sleep, or the heart disease ravaging within. MacBean was so driven, himself, that it never occurred to him that anything might be more important than success, or that success might have a different definition than accumulating wealth, and more wealth, and yet more wealth. Bernstein never complained about being tired or about the disconnect he was discovering between his wealth and his happiness now that he realized he was every bit as mortal as a poor man.

MacBean was approached by a major mutual fund

company within one year of his time as a research assistant under Bernstein. Not only was his reputation growing at KBL, it was also growing on Wall Street. He was Mr. B's shining star, and some influential outsiders learned about the skilled "youngster". The CEO of a mutual fund company called him personally and asked him to consider co-managing a small, emerging high-tech fund. MacBean had climbed to heights unheard of for someone his age and without yet a finance degree. Bernstein found out quickly through the grapevine about this offer, and he called MacBean into his office. Immediately, he doubled MacBean's salary to two thousand a week. MacBean told him he wasn't interested in working anywhere else regardless of the offers, even if it meant more money. He told Bernstein that the Scottish tend to be a very loyal type. Bernstein replied that he would receive a bonus of between ten and twenty thousand semi-annually, depending on the performance of his client's portfolios.

That mutual fund company offered MacBean much more pay, but he knew that a long-term career path at KBL was his goal. Being on track to make one hundred forty-five thousand in the coming year was enough for now, because MacBean knew that sticking with KBL would mean larger payoffs down the road. Being a valued young executive with the most prestigious brokerage house on Wall Street was heady stuff already, but the future was, as the cliché goes, not just bright, but a super nova. Unlike leaving Harvard, leaving KBL was not an option, not for someone aiming for Wall Street's biggest prizes.

In 1971, for the first time since WWII for such a governmental action, President Richard Nixon declared a ninety-day freeze on wages and prices to slow inflation. [(14)]

One late evening after his usual long day, MacBean decided to stop by his old deli and share a Reuben with Mr. Bloomberg. One of his favorite customers at the deli came in and introduced him to his stunning niece. Her name was Penelope Windmire. The only thing more beautiful than her name was Penelope herself. Reddish blonde hair, cream colored complexion, light freckles, and green eyes that made MacBean fully grasp the expression "bedroom eyes". He felt breathless as though someone had sucker-punched him. Totally smitten, he found himself wondering if her freckles grew larger when in the sun. He could imagine himself kissing each and every freckle on that beautiful face.

Penelope had come from Philly to visit her uncle. The relationship began at a fast and furious pace. She moved in with her uncle and she landed a job in the cosmetics department of Saks Fifth Avenue. This made MacBean's apartment conveniently located for them both.

If he was fortunate to see her on a weeknight, it wasn't for long because he worked late and she had an early curfew. At the time, MacBean thought life was close to perfect, not realizing just how little experience he had for someone his age, making him naively unclear on the difference between lust and love or between sex and a committed relationship.

It was spring 1971, and MacBean was twenty-four. Penelope was also a young twenty-year-old. Her parents were strict, and she could not stay overnight at his place. Penelope's uncle, John Witherspoon, followed Penelope's parent's advice by giving her an 11:30 P.M. curfew while living with him. Hell, some parts of New York City didn't come to life until midnight. But MacBean made darn sure when they dated that he brought Penelope home to her uncle's house no later than 11 P.M. just to play it safe, even though he thought it odd, since many New Yorkers are just picking up their dates at 11 P.M. Old blue eyes had it right when he said New York never sleeps.

Because of work and college commitments, MacBean tried

his best to fit in a date with Penelope once during the week and also on a Saturday or Sunday night. Most of the time they would take in dinner and a movie, a concert, or stop by a coffee house , since they shared a love of folk singing. He definitely didn't know at the time he needed more balance between personal and business lives, being so focused on becoming a financial success. His only real friend at the time was Jack Slade, and even he only heard from MacBean every couple of months when MacBean managed to dash off a postcard to 'Nam.

Six months after meeting her, he proposed, and she accepted. MacBean was foolishly thinking they would spend more time together after marriage since they'd be living under the same roof. It was a small wedding with only the immediate families. Seemingly, his hormones had blocked out what he knew very well about Sam Slade and Harvey Bernstein. The higher the rung on the ladder, the less time for anything other than climbing to the next rung.

After the marriage, MacBean left home many mornings before Penelope woke up, and often arrived back home after she was fast asleep. But MacBean felt sure that Penelope understood the demands of his career. Someone else might say that he took her for granted. She started complaining after just two months of marriage. The topic was always that MacBean was away from home all the time and spent no quality time with her. In hindsight, MacBean would come to recognize that she was absolutely right. But, at the time, he just kept telling her to be patient and that he was working hard for the both of them, at KBL and in college classes. That way, they could eventually get ahead in life and not ever have to worry about personal finances. For twenty-year-old Penelope, sacrificing today for a better future tomorrow proved to be too abstract a concept to fully appreciate, as she sat alone every evening watching television and wondering what her unmarried girlfriends were doing that night.

She was also sick of MacBean talking incessantly about financial security. If MacBean had married in his forties, perhaps he would have appreciated her objections to his work schedule. In fact, he had no conception of what a personal life encompassed. Penelope was a nice girl who had great respect for other people. She knew what she wanted much earlier in life than he did, when it came to a personal relationship. She did not care if they were middle or upper class. All she wanted was a husband to spend some time with, not the absent husband that he was. Yet MacBean spent less awake time with her in their nearly two years of marriage than he did when dating, which only confirmed his idea that marriage was better for a successful career than dating!

MacBean's rise to the top of KBL continued, and his paycheck kept escalating, but that didn't solve the problems at home. He bought Penelope a jaguar, two carat diamond earrings, and he often sent her a dozen roses. They wined and dined on Saturday evenings spending three to four hundred dollars for a meal and a night out. As it turned out, the money spent bought no happiness for either of them. What Penelope needed and what MacBean wanted seemed as far apart as ever. What's more, he never, for a single moment, thought she might be right, but rather he felt her to be foolishly naïve. The concept of compromise had not yet occurred to either of them, as often happens with the young.

By the time MacBean was twenty-five and married one year, he was making close to four hundred thousand a year, including bonuses. By then he'd begun to spend money to save their relationship. Spending like a maniac, he was confident he would keep on making more money, and eventually it would be enough to conquer any problems. Without realizing it, he was caught up in a vicious trap. Not saving money any more, he was still certain of his KBL future, and he was betting on it to pull him through the rough times of the relationship.

A few months after the first anniversary, Penelope began

buying expensive wardrobes to fill up her spare time, which was most of her life. Yet MacBean never objected outwardly, feeling it was payment in lieu of guilt.

MacBean tried to talk Penelope into taking some college courses, thinking that it would absorb some of her free time. But Penelope wanted no part in furthering her education. She started taking the train back to Philly to see her parents as often as she could, usually when she had a couple days off in a row. "Why not" she said to MacBean. "I am just a possession to you in your own little financial world". MacBean always responded with declarations of love, and then, in fact, encouraged her to go to Philly as often as she liked, which usually made her madder. Penelope would stare at the latest pile of clothes she'd bought on her most recent shopping binge. "Actions speak louder than your words", she shouted many times. Each felt justified in their feelings and neither had any conception of what the other was talking about. The give and take of a true marriage continued to elude them.

Intellectually, MacBean felt they were miles apart, believing himself, of course, on the upper end, namely because he prioritized his business skills as more important than anything else, but he did recognize that she had what his mum would have called "good, old fashioned common sense." Penelope understood when she did something stupid or counterproductive and she was unlikely to make the same mistake twice. Yet MacBean still didn't understand that working hard to make a marriage work was not the same as just working hard, that making a marriage work might require even more of a commitment than making money. Penelope knew MacBean was a good man and he knew Penelope was a good woman. Still, neither had enough life experience to understand each other on anything other than a surface level.

They were celebrating their second anniversary in 1972 when he received a phone call that Harvey Bernstein had had a massive heart attack. Just under sixty, his lifestyle had caught up with him. MacBean felt a cold shiver go through him. "I'm scared, Penelope: it feels like the beginning of the end, and I don't want it to be". That night MacBean cried in Penelope's arms. She felt closer to MacBean, to the man who might actually need somebody, than she ever had. Yet, in the morning, when she awoke to find him gone off to work, as though it had never happened, she felt a mixture of devastation and anger. MacBean would send her two dozen roses that morning but without a card or a phone call. She threw them into the trash, knowing that it wasn't just Harvey Bernstein facing the beginning of the end.

Because of Bernstein's heart attack, MacBean was now the one in charge, while the older man recovered. He knew that Harvey's misfortune could be his good luck, and he didn't want to let Harvey down. Bernstein's personal staff was great to work with. MacBean was directly thrown into the fire and suddenly was speaking directly to and consulting with Harvey's clients. During Harvey's illness, MacBean even went back to the office on the nights after his college classes to keep up with the pace. Because of the new responsibilities, his pay escalated to around one million a year. MacBean could no longer count the times he'd say to himself, *I told you so* when it came to leaving Harvard.

His ascent at KBL to this salary had happened in less than five years. Yet with all kinds of taxes plus his spending money like a proverbial drunken sailor, he had slacked off in savings. Here he was managing all his clientele's portfolios with literally no time to manage his own. Making a typical rich rookie mistake, he kept thinking he was making so much money that there was no way he'd ever spend it all. Now, both his marriage and his portfolio were suffering.

Six months later Bernstein would be back at work, but he would never be quite the same again. MacBean's relationship with Penelope was strained to the breaking point, and his expensive gifts and dinners no longer satisfied her. In the previous six months, each of them had moved out of and back into the studio apartment three times. MacBean tried to keep his focus on the work ahead of him and not on the essentially empty life they seemed to be living. With Bernstein only working limited hours, combined with MacBean's natural workaholic inclinations, he couldn't help but be secretly glad that his work was demanding all of his time.

When he turned twenty-six, he was essentially running the show for Bernstein, but Penelope finally asked for a divorce. Even having a paycheck nearly equal to Bernstein's meant little to her. She wanted a husband, not a bank account. He was nonetheless proud to be on track to becoming an equal partner to Bernstein per his request to KBL.

When Penelope and MacBean finally divorced, he never saw or spoke with her again. There was no animosity on his part, and he wanted to believe she felt the same. After they decided to go their separate ways, they, in fact, wished each other a genuine best of luck. MacBean would never know what became of Penelope. She did not ask for anything financial from him, but he did feel guilty and thus gave her the assets he had, slightly over one hundred thousand. He also told her to take anything she wanted from the apartment, including jewelry, art, and anything else that might interest her. Although he was unaware of it at the time, this was the beginning of a pattern with MacBean, believing that financial recompense would make up for mistakes made, as if love were nothing more complicated than a contract between two parties, as if he could purchase a dispensation on his guilt, as if Penelope's lonely evenings were wiped away with the stroke of a pen signing over his assets to her.

In November 1972, the Dow closed above 1000 for the first time. (2)

The young man's success on Wall Street had started to make press. Several times a day MacBean would catch himself thinking, *Just twenty-six and I'm considered the youngest up and coming Wall Street wizard. I'm at the top of this privileged world, when I speak the financial world has learned to listen.* In addition to being sought by television for financial soundbites and interviews, MacBean began lecturing at colleges and Fortune 500 company gatherings with the requisite hefty speaker fees. Although his contemporary wunderkinds, Gates and Jobs, would end up accumulating extreme amounts of wealth, much more than MacBean, for their advancements in the high tech industry, JoJo was the first one to accomplish such fame in the Wall Street arena by the age of twenty-six, going from stock clerk to a king of Wall Street in under six years.

JoJo MacBean had made a name for himself and was known by almost every business person of importance. He also became a highly compensated director of other Fortune 500 companies, with permission from the SEC, of course, including Sam Slade's. Kurtzner Brothers LTD., could not be part of the issuing of any prospectuses for the companies on whose boards he sat because to do so would be a conflict of interest. Still, this was sound public relations for the firm.

MacBean kept himself as busy as usual for at least a year after the divorce, with not even a single date. But his lifestyle had changed significantly. He now wore five thousand-dollar suits and smoked eight-dollar cigars. On occasion, he would drop 20K on a suit made by his personal tailor, who came to the office to measure him up, just as he'd always imagined. His mum was getting too old to make his suits, but she always looked over his new tailored ones to give her stamp of approval. MacBean would drop two thousand a week in fancy restaurants eating out late every night at the end of a long work day. But there were moments when he would be sitting alone in the restaurant asking, *Am I happy?* Of course, the expensive bottle of wine at every meal drowned his loneliness most of the time. Yet when he'd arrive at home late, and put his key into the lock, sometimes even imagining someone waited for him on the door's other side, he wondered whether a bottle of cheap wine wouldn't do just as well. Often, as he ate his dinner, he would browse through the financial news that day to see what the people with expertise in his profession were thinking about, and where the economy was heading. This was his way of relaxing, or at least that's what he told himself.

MacBean tried to visit his parents every Sunday for a half hour or so before he'd head into the office to make up his agenda for the coming week. He knew it was only a matter of time before he'd be taking over all of Bernstein's business, and he wanted to ensure both the man and the firm that he could make that transition of power as quickly as possible. It wasn't that MacBean didn't realize he had big shoes to fill at less than half Bernstein's age. Nor did he fail to understand he still had much to learn, or that as good as he was at his job, some of Bernstein's clients would have felt more comfortable if MacBean were a little older with more experience. In other words, MacBean knew he would need to earn their trust, but he also had no doubt he could do so.

Bernstein had accumulated more assets than he could ever spend, once telling MacBean that he could have easily retired at forty, but why should he when he loved what he did? Bernstein was one heck of a teacher and MacBean the perfect student. He absorbed the older man's teachings like the proverbial sponge. Even though MacBean now thought he knew more about the market than the older broker, he had the polish that MacBean still lacked and clients loved. MacBean was so analytical that he came across as a nerd often times: a damn smart nerd but not the kind of man you'd want to spend time with, the kind of man people wanted to be around, wanted to say they were clients of. Harvey Bernstein had perfected those personal skills to a degree that made clients feel grateful to give him their money. MacBean knew he would eventually become more polished and the clients already loved the money he made them, even if not loving the man yet. He would never *be* a Harvey Bernstein when it came to smooth schmoozing with clients, striking that balance between friendship and broker that mixed warm, personal feelings with the lust for cold, impersonal bottom lines.

On the personal side of life, MacBean continued to think he was struggling to get his act together without actually giving that part of his life any real thought or effort, as if it shouldn't require any but ought magically to happen simply because he was successful in one sphere of his life. A phone call on a warm evening in 1972 while he was working late reminded him of this.

"Hello, MacBean? Is that you?"

"Sam! How the heck are you? It's been ages, so busy, I have no excuse. And how's Jack? "

"You know he was going to Nam, right? "

"How could I forget? We had a huge argument over it. I lost that argument same as you did. Didn't he end up in an office, though? I thought he wrote me he was in an office, doing some kind of supply management."

"He wanted combat, he asked for reassignment, MacBean."

"No, not Jack, never, he's a bright boy."

"He was, a bright boy, I mean. Now…"

"Sam, what are you.."

"He's dead, MacBean. My boy. My boy is dead. I killed him."

"I can't believe it. But Sam, you told him not to enlist!"

"But he knew I'd be proud of him if he did. He wrote me a letter telling me that he wanted to make me proud. As if. ."

"Are you sure, Sam? Are you sure?"

"He's been killed; he was actually starting on his way home; it was a chopper crash. My boy. My boy." The phone clicked off. MacBean dialed Sam's number, but it was a busy signal.

He called home and asked his father what he should do. "Go to Sam, of course. He needs you". But MacBean also knew he had an important client meeting in the morning that could make the difference between taking over KBL in six months or not for another year or perhaps not even until Bernstein retired. Instead MacBean wrote a letter to Sam, a beautiful letter telling him of all the kind things that Jack had done for MacBean and for others. He promised himself he would attend the funeral, which he did, and at which he told Sam that he'd always be there for him, never more than a phone call away. Sam didn't call MacBean then, but instead threw himself into his work with more fervor than ever, working even longer hours, as if growing profits could drown his regrets and lessen his sorrow. MacBean never called Sam. *Work's the best thing for him right now.* It wasn't until later in that year that Sam called MacBean and asked him to come over to spend Jack's birthday with him. MacBean found a broken man had taken over the Sam Slade he once knew. It was a difficult conversation for MacBean, not knowing whether it best to shout at Sam to "buck up", or to allow Sam's sadness to envelop both of them. He left there feeling useless, which was not a feeling he liked. He would lose touch with Sam until a day around six months later when he found himself sitting on the board of Slade Enterprises as a director, and voted for Sam's removal as CEO as part of a takeover. It's business, Sam, just business. By then, Sam had worked himself into a total breakdown physically and emotionally and was not surprised by the takeover or the vote. But that it had been unanimous caused him a great deal of pain that MacBean could see in Sam's face. When Sam said to MacBean, "You could have just abstained, my boy, that's all I would have expected," MacBean at first didn't understand how Sam couldn't see *this was business*. That night at home, MacBean called his mother to talk with her about Sam's comment. Claire did not treat her son kindly that night and like a child feeling sorry only for himself, he cried himself to sleep. When he woke the next morning, he remembered his mother's words and he told himself, she doesn't understand how business works. But a still small voice answered, maybe she understands it all too well.

MacBean was now making about one million dollars a month at KBL before taxes, and by now as addicted to his work as any addict to his drug of choice. But another addiction had begun to show its ugly face, the addiction to the money itself. He had no one to share the wealth with at the end of his eighteen-hour days, and yet he continued at that pace in spite of realizing full well that he was a very lonely man.

One war ended with the January 27, 1973 Paris Peace Accords, and another "war" began with the January 11, 1973 start of the seventh worst bear market in stock exchange history. The Bear would last until December 6, 1974 and ultimately result in a 45% loss. [(15)]

Now in charge of fifteen-hundred client accounts, MacBean had joined several prestigious business organizations and dining clubs, including the Twin Oaks Club, better known as the Manhattan Millionaire's Club, with a fifty-thousand-dollar initiation fee. MacBean made that back in no time once he joined, because several of the members became his clients. It was at that club in late '72 that he met Brandy Seymour, a beautiful blue-eyed blond with long, flowing hair and even longer legs. Their relationship was an accident waiting to happen.

Brandy had never worked a day in her life. Her father, Gerald Seymour, was the owner of Seymour Solutions Inc. with over two thousand employees. The company had three, around the clock, shifts a day plus overtime and weekends.

Needless to say, Mr. Seymour had already become one of MacBean's clients when he had joined the Twin Oaks Club.

MacBean was immediately attracted to Brandy with a desire that made it impossible for him not to want to possess her totally. Without realizing it, he was participating in a bit of trophy hunting as well, since Brandy was the topic of much competition having made it known she wasn't going to "settle" for less than the lifestyle she desired. Unfortunately, as it turned out, MacBean won her, thanks to her dear old dad. Mr. Seymour made it known that MacBean was up and coming and would continue to keep his daughter financially secure. . and then some. Being daddy's little girl, Brandy paid attention. In hindsight, she might have fared better if she had listened to her mummy, a woman who knew a work addict when she saw one, having lived with one in the kind of sterile marriage she'd hoped her daughter would avoid. But just as Mrs. Seymour had initially convinced herself she'd sincerely been attracted to the highest bidder, so did Brandy convince both herself and MacBean that she'd fallen in love.

MacBean refused to believe that Brandy had her eye on him only for financial reasons, even though he was infatuated with her primarily for prestigious ones. It mimicked an arranged royal marriage. The princess would became Princess with a capital P and the Prince would get the woman who could have chosen any man on earth.

Christmas Eve of 1973, MacBean's birthday, his mother Claire MacDyer died unexpectedly. It wasn't unexpected for Lonnie, but Claire had made him promise to keep her illness from their son. When the end came, Lonnie was with her but MacBean had hurried to the hospital only to be just minutes too late. Looking back, MacBean thought to himself it was the best time for her to go because the wake and the burial were the day after Christmas and he wouldn't have to lose any work. Although he knew that was a selfish thing to think, he never thought about his Dad needing some of his son's time to help his mourning. Yet MacBean being there at all made Lonnie feel grateful. He was as sad as any son would be, and he knew his dad would now be lonely without his Claire. MacBean tried to imagine what it would be like to have a wife that felt like part of yourself, someone to rely on through anything and who would love you forever, genuinely forever, literally forever, always and forever. *Why couldn't I find that someone? Was it easier for a poor man? Was that the trick? Start poor and become rich later?* Though he wondered these things, he still didn't make the connection between Claire's passing and his Dad's possible need to spend time with his son.

Although surprising to Brandy and MacBean but not to those who genuinely knew them, their sex life in marriage was lousy. Before the marriage, Brandy was quite passionate. Once the objective was achieved, she became less so. Her idea of foreplay was to spend money and MacBean's idea of romance was to make it. It was actually close to an ideal situation in some ways. Brandy acted the spoiled brat who didn't care in the least how many hours MacBean worked as long as she had carte blanche to spend. Brandy was actually just acting the role her mother had so aptly played out for her, including hiding any sincere feelings of neglect or need deep within. MacBean could never imagine a woman who wouldn't mind being left alone most evenings until late in the night so carte blanche to spend seemed an even trade. And yet, a nagging sense of something missing in his life kept creeping into his thoughts in the moments just before sleep would overtake him. He certainly never imagined Brady would jeopardize his financial largesse by having affairs, let alone one-night stands, with other men at the Club. When he realized what was happening, he found himself embarrassed but not hurt, more concerned with his good business name than with her actual fidelity. MacBean saw this as the equivalent to a good curve ball being thrown at him, but it being only strike two. So much so that he ignored the situation for another year, until she made the mistake of fooling around with one of MacBean's clients. Losing face was never acceptable, and would make his second divorce necessary at age twenty-nine.

Brandy and her attorney took him for everything that he had and some of what he would have. Again, it did not seem to matter to MacBean because he felt he had plenty of time to make up for the money that his naivete lost. His reasoning was that he would simply start all over and be successful again. *Why wouldn't I?* Ironically, he became so asset poor, he himself wouldn't have qualified as an KBL client.

1976 marked the U.S. Bicentennial. It also marked the year that two Steves, Jobs and Wozniak, officially formed Apple Computer [16]***. Microsoft was created one year earlier in 1975.*** [17]

When Harvey Bernstein passed away in 1976, MacBean had already been co- managing most of his boss's clients for three years, with many of them solely his clients in all but name. He didn't care a whit whose name got the credit as long as he earned a fair percentage. MacBean had evolved into a rather unique businessman. He pretended not to care about credit as long as the bottom line of his bank account was growing. Even MacBean found it odd that his ego didn't need the stroking that it seemed some egos did. But when he thought about Sam Slade or Harvey Bernstein, he knew they also weren't in it for fame, but for money. But as time went on, MacBean found himself asking, *Is it really just the money? It's not fame, that's a nice perk, but it's fame that leads to making more money. But isn't it supposed to be for what money can get you? So far it hasn't gotten me much that matters, except. . .except what?*

Bernstein left MacBean with quite a list of wealthy clientele, which he expanded on because of his own reputation, proving why fame was important. In fact, his clientele list was growing at an alarming pace. He now had six staff under him and anticipated that would keep growing. Three of his assistants were Wharton graduates, two from Babson, and one was a graduate from Bernard Baruch College. The staff was well-trained, and, as a team, they were on top of the world.

In the coming year, two sheiks from Kuwait became his clients, as did a Japanese emperor, a Brazilian president and several rulers from small countries, including King Gustav of Sweden. There were some internationally known figureheads, such as members of the British Parliament. He also added about a hundred and fifty of the wealthiest businessmen in the world, many of them coming from Europe. Now the KBL client list included eight-hundred executives in Fortune 500 companies and about two-hundred fifty of the upper echelon of privately held companies. Some of these privately-held companies were owned by well-known physicians and prominent lawyers. To that client list was added a scattering of movie stars and professional athletes. MacBean started saying, "When KBL speaks, Wall St. listens. When MacBean speaks, the whole world listens." Yet it wasn't ego that made him say that, it was simple, honest, delight in his success. And soon, the failed marriage with Brandy and the loss of most of his assets at the time, faded in memory. So also did any lessons learned, almost as if making money had a strangely amnesiac affect, like most other addictions.

As the clientele kept on growing, MacBean busily started recruiting some of the best brokers and stock researchers from the competition on Wall Street. Most of the ones he sought ended up at KBL, even if it cost him more than a 100K per year per person. He knew from his own experience that the right people on your team could earn far more than they cost. The fact that the competition didn't have them either was an added bonus. MacBean was building a company with the best business minds in the brokerage sector. When he told his Dad about this, Lonnie called KBL the New York Yankees of all the brokerage houses. MacBean thought of it as more like Super-MacBean was building his own Marvel universe of superheroes.

The professionals began handling the day to day tasks of servicing clientele. When clients would fly in from anywhere in the world, MacBean would meet with them personally, face to face. These meetings took time, but it was important that MacBean made those clients feel that they were very important to both KBL and to him, which they actually were. But MacBean could no longer handle any of the trades because of his responsibilities overseeing the ever-growing empire he had created. He constantly networked leads from other clients with new clients needing a liquid net worth of at least ten million dollars.

Three hundred new clients brought the existing list up to eighteen hundred in his first year of total control, a twenty percent increase. Billions of new dollars were coming into KBL because of MacBean and his team. It seemed that KBL managed more money than the U.S. Mint. The fact that he didn't exercise, ate lousy food, and slept less than any human needed, still hadn't dawned on him as cause of concern. It was always something to think about "in the future".

In more than one way, his largest client was Bucklin W. Fullam III. He was a heavy man pushing near four-hundred pounds. His son, Bucklin W. Fullam IV, by his own right, was also a client. He was huge, but not nearly the size of his dad. MacBean had nicknamed the two of them Big Bucks and Little Bucks. He hadn't intended to let them know of their informal monikers, but when they overheard someone refer to them that way, they immediately went to MacBean and asked, "What's the story with the Big Bucks and Little Bucks?" MacBean stammered a bit and started to apologize at which time both the Bucks burst out laughing. "We're just ribbing you, MacBean. We love the nicknames! Fact is, we're having new business cards made with 'em!" Shortly thereafter, they bought out a small restaurant chain, revamped it into a BBQ place, and renamed the chain Big Bucks and Little Bucks, with the logo of a big hog and a small pig. MacBean admired both of the men because they didn't let any false vanity keep them from making money. The food was also especially good. Big Bucks told MacBean the chain used his granddaddy Vernon's recipe for their sauce and his grandma Etha's recipe for the cornbread.

Big Bucks and Little Bucks were among the wealthiest clients at KBL. Their personal net worth was in the billions, and Forbes Magazine listed the two of them in the top five wealthiest people in the world. At KBL, their assets held were sixty percent of their total net worth. These two were major stockholders in an international auto parts company called International Motors Inc., which was listed on the New York Stock Exchange. Bernstein had played a big part in taking their company public. This made the Fullam's a not insignificant fortune. They were loyal to KBL because Bernstein took Big Bucks and Little Bucks from rich to filthy rich.

In the mid-seventies, some of the KBL clients, who were professional athletes, had their own sneaker lines, and MacBean had even appeared on a few commercials for some of his clients' companies, usually as the non-athlete who could become like the professional athlete – all because of the sneakers he wore. Of course, he did the commercials gratis, which helped to make JoJo MacBean a household name. Not for the fame but because of what fame meant - more clients and more money.

MacBean was now traveling the country about two weeks a month and internationally three to four times a year. He spoke to major audiences at least two Saturdays a month, earning a lecture fee of two-hundred thousand. He figured if a company could afford that fee, they were clientele potential. And if already a client of KBL, he knew they could afford the fee.

There were always newspapers, magazines, and national TV networks calling to interview him. Personal time was literally nonexistent, with every waking moment being work time.

SUNDAYS WITH LONNIE

It was a time of particular upheaval in every sector, including the resignation of a President, but upheaval in the technology sector would be an understatement, as if a molehill were getting ready not to become a mere mountain, but setting the stage for eventual Himalayas status. The computer era was taking giant leaps forward. As a result, the technology funds that had previously been a gamble, were now becoming far less so. If someone put a small portion of their money in a technology fund, they would have likely made a fortune on that small investment. MacBean had advised his clients that were interested in technology funds to only place a small portion of their portfolio in this sector, because it still felt like a risk, and KBL did not like to take risks. But MacBean also realized that such a small, limited but targeted investment in the technology sector could yield remarkable returns. As it turned out, the technology funds and investments in technology stocks would yield double-digit returns for several years. Most of the clients who had the steady nerves to make those small investments made fortunes in the technology sector without losing much on the small investments that didn't work out. It was as if a technology stock either went bust or did very, very well. And very, very well usually outran the investments lost on the busts if the broker had done his research, as MacBean and his team had.

His competent team now included the latest gurus in technology, and KBL was making more profits than ever. Still, MacBean never made a move just with a good feeling, only by having a high degree of certainty based on social and economic trends and the foresight of his tech gurus.

By mid-1977, MacBean's clientele list had grown to over twenty-two hundred, with over a hundred and fifty of those clients worth over a half a billion dollars, and twenty percent of those over one billion.

His team at KBL was now larger than the rest of the brokers' staffs in both size and earnings. MacBean had risen to fame outside KBL, even outside Wall Street, yet he was only on the cusp of his thirtieth birthday. The wealthy were calling KBL and asking for that young phenom with the funny Scottish name to handle their account.

KBL had to raise the requirements for giving him a new client to a minimum of fifty million in assets, with at least half to be invested with KBL. If a potential client couldn't meet the new standards, they were referred to other KBL brokers. In short, MacBean had become a gravy train to the other brokers who fed off his cast-offs.

MacBean was also now becoming connected politically with four governors, eight senators, and twenty-seven Congressmen on his client list. Although all were wealthy, KBL made some exceptions to the assets requirements because one could never tell when a politician might prove useful for a favor. Lobbyists were also on his client list, which helped him to keep abreast of the latest patents and the newest drugs, with that knowledge being gained before they entered the markets. MacBean made sure he stayed on the right side of the razor thin line between gossip and trading on insider information. But it was a line growing increasingly difficult for both MacBean and his team to locate. When his first invitation to a White House function arrived, MacBean was excited to show it to his dad. *Imagine, the son of immigrants dining at the White House with President and Mrs. Ford.*

Yet, as MacBean made his clients wealthier, he still had little control over his own financial situation. Working hard but living fast and spending, spending, and more spending, along with stress, stress, and more stress, trapped him in a constant cycle of monthly deficits. At age thirty-two, with two divorces in less than four years, he found himself asking more frequently than ever *What good is an invitation to the White House if I have no one to share it with?* His earnings were growing, but they were merely subsidizing two failed marriages. When he was married, he had no time for his wife. When he wasn't married, he had no time for friends or his parents. *Isn't being driven supposed to be an asset? Is it possible I'm wrong about that?*

After one of these questioning times, MacBean vowed to devote every Sunday to his dad, unless, of course, he was on a business trip out of town. Unfortunately, there were a lot of business trips. But Lonnie told him, "Don't worry about what you can't do, just do what you can."

On the Sundays he was in town, he and his dad would begin their visit by going to church together. The fact that MacBean went back to church on Sundays helped him start to restore some of his faith in God, because once he left his parents' house to go to college, he stopped attending church. He called his dad every Saturday night to remind him about church the next morning. MacBean knew he needn't do that, but it became part of his own ritual for winding himself down from his workweek.

After church, they would dine at one of the finest restaurants in New York City. His dad, Lonnie, always suggested they go to Bloomberg's for brunch, but MacBean said he wanted to treat his dad to a brunch he'd never treat himself to. MacBean felt awkward about going to Bloomberg's because, as little as he visited his dad, he visited Mr. Bloomberg even less. At breakfast, father and son would talk and read The *New York Times* together and then go for a stroll in Central Park, if the weather was nice. Then they'd go back to Dad's house and play some cribbage and watch a baseball or football game. Once in a while, MacBean would take his Dad to a classical concert or to a Yankees game. Lonnie would cook them a light supper, and they'd finish the evening with a beer together before MacBean would head home. Neither MacBean or Lonnie talked much about work. Lonnie still worked part time a few afternoons, as bartender at a small neighborhood pub called "O'Hara's". Dad was happy to still be healthy and make a few bucks working, even if it was at a bar with an Irish name! He still kept his little house as neat as a pin, just as Claire had. MacBean had once bought him a Cadillac, and he made MacBean return it to the car dealer, which he was secretly glad to do since he'd bought it on credit. Dad still had many friends in the neighborhood and was invited by those friends to dinner many times but seldom went. He had always liked a couple of beers and an order of fish and chips on Fridays after work with the boys and being home by 7 P.M.

Eventually MacBean began to feel as though his Sundays with Dad were his only "real" days, and all the others felt like the scene outside as seen from inside a speeding train. His Sundays and their simplicity began to heal him in a way he hadn't even recognized he needed. He felt reconnected again to that kid who dreamed of Wall St. success because it was for him the epitome of the American dream. Lately, MacBean wasn't so sure anybody's dream ought to include seventy or so hours a week of work, no matter how much money it might earn them.

Looking back on his first twelve years at KBL, MacBean knew it was the two-year period of Sundays with his Dad that he treasured more than any other time. He couldn't recall many individual moments in those twelve KBL years, but he remembered almost every Sunday's events – where they ate, what they ate, the game they watched, and what they talked about. They both felt regret that MacBean hadn't started those Sunday visits earlier, when Claire was still alive. MacBean had meant to, but he lived his life for his work instead of working for a living. Dad always reminded him that Mum was in heaven looking down on them every Sunday smiling as her Lonnie and JoJo made time for each other.

As the two-year period came near its end, MacBean couldn't help but think, *why couldn't I do with a woman what I did with my dad?* The wheels began to turn a little, but not yet enough. MacBean did realize he was still not a happy person, except for the Sundays he spent with his dad. Dad was one of the happiest persons he knew, yet Lonnie lived a simple life. Once, when MacBean told his dad he was sorry he hadn't spent enough time with him and Mum after leaving home, Lonnie said, "JoJo, part of life is living and learning. We all have to find our own way. Some people never find the way, and that is unfortunate." MacBean could never tell for sure if Dad meant him. MacBean told him often that he admired him more than any other man, not because he was his father but because he had been a great father, a great husband, and a great friend to so many others. And one time he had added "I think maybe you are the true American success, Dad." Lonnie could tell by the way his son had said it, softly and sincerely and with a little surprise, that he should not disagree with such a self- revelation.

Every Sunday upon leaving, Lonnie hugged MacBean in the only genuine bear hugs he had ever received and promised himself never to forget them.

Despite the money MacBean was earning, his dad would only allow him to pay for brunch if the supper and beer were on him, always the proud Scotsman. Until the Sunday that Lonnie insisted on paying because he was bringing someone with him and he wanted to go to Bloomberg's Deli. Lonnie was a proud and independent man and seemed to MacBean not to be at all interested in dating after Claire died. Yet a year after her death, he had invited a woman to have brunch with them. MacBean was flabbergasted. When they entered into Bloomberg's, he saw a woman around his dad's age with a lovely, warm smile, and he felt a tremendous wave of envy of his dad. Here was someone not after money but only after someone's love and companionship. *How did my dad get so lucky not once, but possibly twice?!* Immediately after sitting down in the booth, MacBean saw the woman sitting in a nearby booth staring at him. He could only stare back as both of them were speechless at seeing the other. It was Rivers who stood up and approached him.

"Well, if it isn't the boy wonder himself. How are you, MacBean?"

"What are you doing here? I mean, in Bloomberg's? "

"Eating my usual order of omelet with latkes. And on my way to Columbia's library for some research."

"Oh Jeez, do they still have time for anything other than protesting?"

"It's a nasty job, but somebody had to do it. I'm finishing up my thesis on"

"Don't tell me, male castration, right? That's what I remember."

"You were a sweet, but naïve, kid. Seems you've become a sour, rich guy. Too bad." Rivers turned around and began walking back to her booth to sit down. MacBean got up and stopped her, turning her to face him and said, "I'm sorry, I have no idea why I reacted that way. Yes, I do. You hurt me, Rivers, you really hurt me."

"I know that, and I'm sorry my hot headedness got the better of me. But you had an empty head back then, truly empty of everything except numbers, and how to make money with those numbers. Although I can't deny you've become pretty good at it."

"It's more than numbers, a lot more. Anyway, I'm sorry I was, how'd you put it, 'empty headed'. I mean that."

"And I'm sorry I didn't want to give you a second chance. Guess we were both pretty stupid kids". Rivers then returned to her booth and sat down.

MacBean walked to the booth and asked her, "Do you come here often?"

"You don't need a line, MacBean, we already know each other, remember?"

"I meant the question seriously. Do you come to Bloomberg's often? I used to work here, remember?"

"Of course, I do, you told me often enough. But I met Sol Bloomberg because he and my father both serve on a committee to build a Holocaust Memorial and Museum down in D.C."

"Bloomberg? This deli's owner? On a D.C. committee?"

"You've been so busy making all your money, you somehow missed that Sol Bloomberg is also a wealthy man. He just doesn't need the world to know it."

"I wish he'd been here today. I came to see him but found out he's not feeling well."

"It's more than not feeling well, MacBean. You'd know that if you'd called him once in a while."

"What are you talking about? What's wrong with him?"

"It's not for me to say. I've got to head back now." With that, Rivers rose from the booth and started to walk out. She turned back to MacBean and said, "I told you once to go fuck yourself. Now I'm telling you to go find yourself, because you're lost, MacBean. In spite of all your fancy trappings, it's a lost man who doesn't know one of his oldest and supposedly dearest friends is quite ill. And if you ever do find yourself, then, but only then, give me a call." She handed MacBean a card from her pocket with her Columbia University phone number.

"You could put him in an empty room and lock him up, and he'd think of some way to make money"–
Jan. 1982 WSJ quote said to be about Alan Greenspan, but often thought to really be about JoJo MacBean.

Lonnie passed away in 1980, when MacBean was almost thirty-four. This simple old Scotsman had so many people pay their respects at his funeral that MacBean felt not only humbled but sad at his own life. It was one of the largest funerals MacBean had ever seen. And each friend told him a different story of how Lonnie had helped them. Someone said to him, "Your dad has left a true legacy. He taught us all how to help others the way he helped us, by giving of yourself when somebody needs it most." MacBean realized he no longer had a single family member in America, at least that he knew of. Oh, there were aunts, uncles, and cousins in Scotland, but he'd never met them. The void left by his dad's death seemed surprisingly vast to MacBean. *Losing a parent is always traumatic, but why does losing just that one day a week with Dad make me feel so alone?*

It seemed to MacBean as though he'd lost both his parents in a short time. Yet he was taught to always think positive, so he tried to focus on how many other men made millions of dollars by his age. Of course, he had also lost millions more than most had by his age due to two expensive divorces. In the morning, MacBean would vow to himself to work on his net worth. But by evening, he had spent more than he planned on something or other. He purchased a yacht to entertain some of his clients, but that was a business deduction. He also bought a Porsche and a Jaguar, which were decidedly not deductions. And yet they stayed most of the time in the garage, as he seldom had any time to drive simply for the joy of driving. In the mornings, MacBean would chastise himself for wasting so much money the previous day. It was an attempt to build a life full of possessions rather than relationships. *Possessions never make me feel guilty for not spending time with them, possessions never ask more of me than I can give, possessions never made me question my commitment to my job. And losing a possession never leaves a hole in your heart that might never be filled.* He didn't know yet to add that you can never climb into bed with one, unless of course it was the expensive goose down mattress he'd just purchased from Denmark.

But even the joy of that wore off after a week or so. Late one evening, MacBean called Bloomberg's. Rivers accusation had added to his overall uneasy feeling.

"Hello, is Mr. Bloomberg in? This is an old friend of his, JoJo MacBean."

"I'm sorry, Mr. MacBean, but Mr. Bloomberg is now in a nursing home, BriarVille Manor, on the upper West Side."

MacBean stood with the phone in hand frozen for a few minutes, before putting it back in its cradle. He called information and eventually reached the nursing home.

"Yes, my name is JoJo MacBean, and I'm needing to check that you have a Sol Bloomberg there at BriarVille. Yes, yes, I'll wait. You do? When do you allow visitors? Oh, great. Can you tell me, are you allowed to tell me, what is Mr. Bloomberg ailing from?"

"We can't share that directly with you. But we can tell you that Mr. Bloomberg is in the early dementia ward."

MacBean again hung up the phone, sat down on the bed, and began to cry. He was unsure if he was crying for Mr. Bloomberg or for himself having let go of the old man so easily and quickly, not even knowing he was failing, let alone now in a home. When he realized he was crying for himself as much as for Sol, he cried even harder, knowing that the old deli owner would most definitely not think MacBean a mensch. He never did visit him, however, as he knew he was not strong enough to withstand being unrecognized by him.

How ironic. I'm a powerful man, yet I feel like a weak one,

not being brave enough to visit him. I wonder if Rivers would find my self-awareness admirable or my selfishness despicable? Hah, like I don't know the answer to that!

HIGH RISK TO NO RISK

MacBean had started learning all he could about technology and computers at Manhattan College, but about this time he began increasing his time spent on it, not just the financial aspects but the nuts and bolts, or in this case things like motherboards and CPUs and how they actually worked. The innovations and improvements were taking place at an alarming pace that the world had seldom seen. The advancements were so fast in this industry that everything was outdated within one to two years. MacBean studied computers and their components any chance he had after work, even managing to squeeze in more college courses in electrical engineering. He had been a wunderkind of Wall St., but in those classes, he was the old man, even though he clearly still had nerd stamped on his forehead. But this technology intrigued him. He knew he wanted to play a big part in the beginning of the high-tech era that was emerging right before his eyes.

High-tech companies were diversifying and specializing in manufacturing specific components, and he wanted to obtain as much knowledge as he could about the software and hardware in the industry. Many of these new companies coming aboard were listed on the stock exchange, especially the NASDAQ. These companies usually needed investment dollars to be raised, and then stock would be issued to investors who had the money to take a higher risk in some of these high-tech startups. These investors met the standards for risk investing because the amount each investor put up, although it was a lot, was minor compared to their vast portfolio. Of course, if the well calculated risk paid off, the higher the reward for those who invested. With the knowledge MacBean had, and the knowledge he continued to gain; he could play a major role in taking some high-tech companies public. He didn't feel he was adding to his plate, just having a little dessert.

In his position at KBL, everyone in the company listened to his ideas regarding all business matters, including the technology field. KBL was still a very conservative company compared to the other brokerage firms. In the past, the firm concentrated on providing conservative and lower risk type investments to its clientele. Yet thanks to the wonderful research teams at KBL, the average return on a client's investments beat all the average indictors of the market. The firm's wealthy clientele continued to be extremely happy.

Because of his increasing knowledge in the evolution of the computer industry, he convinced all the brokers at KBL that the technology field was not just a safer bet, but it was now risky not to have some tech investments. Therefore, brokers could not exceed a maximum of four percent of a client's total portfolio in high tech stocks but were encouraged to at least meet that threshold. Of course, there were some exceptions because some clients insisted on risking ten percent of their liquidity in the technology field, and others, the "old guard" clients, still didn't want any of their assets going into high tech.

But KBL had smart brokers, and MacBean knew they were more than adequately trained for recommending the low risk investments. Now they were gaining knowledge in the high-tech field, and they felt comfortable bringing up to clients the new technology investments that were available. MacBean often reminded the brokers to always listen to their client's respective concerns so that no client ever felt disregarded, but that a broker also had an obligation to assist the client in understanding when a trend was on the verge of becoming a safer risk, meaning buy low and expect to sell high.

By 1982, MacBean was on the board of directors of even more Fortune 500 companies. He had transitioned out of direct management of clientele accounts to avoid conflicts of interest. The scores he made from taking a company public were far more than he could ever make as a broker. KBL simplified this matter in 1981, when MacBean was finally made president and CEO of the company at thirty-four. Some of the brokers joked about whether or not MacBean's fascination with computers was merely financial or was related to the fact that he worked such long hours he was clearly more cyborg than human. But no cyborg would have spent the evening of his promotion telling his deceased dad he wished he were there to celebrate together with a big bowl of popcorn and a beer down at O'Hara's.

In reality, he still had overall control of clients, but the brokers under his watch took care of the day-to-day affairs. The company realized he was developing into someone who could cultivate and maintain solid client relationships. MacBean had known he would never be Harvey Bernstein, and he wasn't. But he was JoJo MacBean, somewhat socially awkward, nerdy, but brilliant. And there was no other CEO or billionaire that could ever claim to work harder.

He established his new team focused on technology with young leaders in the fast-rising high-tech sector. He had several computer geniuses who knew all the components of computers and on top of the latest terminology being developed in the software and hardware field. Before taking a company public, MacBean would study their main product and the services they provided, and he would then examine their potential for future growth. He knew that if he could raise the proper working capital, by taking that company public, that it had to be a strong calculated risk. The goal was to maximize the potential profits for these investors based on MacBean's research. Each prospectus that his team organized went to the Securities and Exchange Commission (SEC). MacBean hired international

CPA firms to prepare the projected financial statements in the prospectus. The major law firms helped with the legal terminology in order to get the prospectus approved by the SEC. This was all part of the initial offering. The lawyers and the CPAs had to make the potential client realize that any future offering comes with risks and uncertainty. This was part of the standard language of a prospectus. That prospectus then had to be approved by this governing body, and then the capital could be raised with the issue of stock in the company that was about to go public. There was no shortage of potential investors and the KBL offerings were sold out quickly to both KBL clientele and non-clientele. The capital raised for these infant companies was crucial because of the glitches they ran into when developing their product. If these companies weren't taken public successfully, they would have been out of business in no time, due to the shortage of capital needed to develop their product. In regards to all the infant high-tech companies, many failed because the proper capital was not raised, or the product was just not good enough. If the initial research was done properly, meaning by KBL, to get these companies launched successfully, about 80 percent of those that failed might not have.

KBL and MacBean made a lot of money on any initial offering tendered. In some cases, there was also a second and third offering to raise the working capital the companies needed to get their product to market. For each successful offering completed, MacBean personally made over two million a pop.

KBL did about thirty-five offerings in the next few years, and thirty-three of them were successful. That was an unmatched track record on Wall St. The costs of the two failures were well absorbed by the thirty-three successes. And naturally, when clients made money, so did KBL, and so did JoJo MacBean.

3

WALL STREET CONQUERING
1985 – 2002

The market began 1985 at 1198 and ended in 2002 at 8341.

It was now 1985, and MacBean was thirty-eight. He had spun off one of the high-tech offerings at KBL by purchasing a portion of the company and renaming it Triton Consulting Enterprises. Triton would become well known in its own short time. This company did consulting for many small to medium sized high-tech companies. Triton also managed internal affairs for these customers. Some of the high-tech staff at KBL transferred to Triton at MacBean's request before taking Triton public.

Because MacBean was now involved with two companies and with some of the employees that moved over from the investment side of KBL to Triton, he thought it might attract attention from the SEC because it looked like KBL and Triton were related companies, a decided "no-no" by security industry standards. Even though he was still a registered broker and president and CEO of KBL, MacBean asked the securities attorney how to best handle this situation to avoid possible problems and conflicts.

A former CEO of KBL himself, Irving R. Shatz, also a lawyer, was asked if MacBean could convey all of his interests in Triton to Shatz's long time mistress, Ronnie Leclair, who knew nothing about a high-tech consulting business. Of course, she would get a handsome salary of one and a half million dollars a year from Triton Consulting Inc. Shatz was happy about that because it would mean less money out of his pocket for her support. Shatz was a large help in funneling the money made by Triton into KBL. Once Ronnie was on board, MacBean made sure that Triton still showed a modest profit after all expenses. In addition to Ronnie's nice salary, Irving bought her a Bentley to drive around in.

Irving's second cousin, Saul Epstein, was the exclusive lawyer for KBL and Triton. These were Saul's only clients. The relationship between Irving and Saul was never disclosed to the SEC. So, in reality, Saul was not an independent lawyer, even though Epstein's law firm collected the monies from the billings to these two companies for their legal services rendered. Then Epstein would receive some handsome paychecks. Saul had quite a staff of lawyers in his law firm plus a few paralegals to boot. His law firm billed Triton and KBL over two million dollars a month for legal services rendered. That was certainly a bundle from only two clients.

Triton Consulting now had a staff of sixty high-tech hardware and software employees, and, of course, MacBean was running the company, just not on paper. The conflict was overcome the way many Wall St. firms would have overcome it at that time, by circumventing the SEC rules. Of course, KBL also funneled much of the money Triton made in various ways. MacBean's greed was at an all-time high now, and his ethics were cloudy enough for him to hear another broker refer to him as "Mr. not-so Clean". He felt he was safe from any legal action as long as he could honestly say that all income made by both companies was fully claimed for tax purposes. Between KBL's continued growth and Triton's emergence in the consulting industry, there were not enough hours in his day.

Even the dinner at the club involved one or more of his staff, and/or clientele, so he could write off some of these expenses, as well as use the time productively. He was the largest spender at the club by far and would tell himself this was his way of relaxing even though it was shop talk all evening. If MacBean were dining alone, he would eat between nine and ten PM, but the club would often stay open extra hours just for him. All the workers, including waiters and waitresses, were tipped well for doing so. Most of the white-gloved wait staff made close to two thousand dollars in tips in a good week. That was more than the average business person made per week. Smaller meals at the club ran MacBean or KBL over five hundred with one or two people joining him for those occasions. When he would raise his glass for a toast to future financial success, he did not fail to recognize his was a life envied by millions. He also did not fail to ask himself, with increasing regularity, why he felt such dread putting his key into the lock of his empty apartment. The habit of having a second drink stiff enough to knock himself out and call it sleep had risen to an addiction.

Triton was hitting sales of over sixty million dollars a year by 1985, and that was only its third year in business. Outside of the payroll, the legal fees and monies funded to KBL for the consulting, fees were Triton's largest expenses. He was forty-one and making approximately thirty million a year. He now had a vacation home in Martha's Vineyard to which he went three times in five years, but he also allowed staff to use it for their families and some of his clientele at cost. He had furnished the house with three hundred thousand dollars' worth of artwork and had also designed and overseen the installation of the high-tech security system himself. With federal, state, and local taxes on top of gasoline taxes and sales taxes, MacBean figured he supported the economy sixty percent in taxes while keeping forty percent for himself.

He indulged in a new luxury car every six months, often with less than five thousand miles on each. The Scotsman in MacBean had officially perished.

In October, 1985, when visiting a client's office, MacBean

noticed a stunning young woman named Angela Cummings. A young attorney the client had recently added to his staff, she was just twenty-six, having graduated a year earlier from law school. He fell for Angela the moment she caught his eye. She was intelligent, ambitious, and pulling down about eighty grand a year. He asked her first for coffee, second to lunch, and third to dinner. The ensuing six months of dating were exciting and fun. They could actually talk business together, or they'd go to Broadway plays or Yankee games. They were cited in social columns as a beautiful couple about town with style, money, and successful careers. They enjoyed sharing activities, something which MacBean had not experienced with Penelope or Brandy. Angela had even joined him for some late dinners at the club after a long work day.

MacBean figured that because of what he thought was Angela's own strong work ethic, their marriage would be a stronger one than his previous ones. She understood the demands of business and the time required to succeed. Angela also had a firm grasp of the current economic environment. MacBean was imagining he'd finally found a life partner in this woman, someone his equal in intelligence and ambition.

He was also flattered that someone nearly fifteen years his junior would want to be his wife. Of course, he wasn't so naïve he didn't know his money was of some importance, but Angela could make her own living, so surely his financial situation wasn't the only attraction. They were married at St. Patrick's Cathedral with every seat taken. Over a thousand people attended the reception, held in all three of the banquet rooms at the Waldorf. It cost over two hundred fifty thousand dollars, for which MacBean picked up the tab. Because he was so busy with KBL and Triton, he could only afford a week away; the newlyweds didn't have much of a honeymoon. It was a week in Hawaii, and Angela begged him to extend the honeymoon another week. He couldn't do that, and thus they had their first married argument. They argued for three days until finally it was decided that Angela would stay on another week while MacBean flew home alone. What a way to start a marriage was all MacBean could think of on the plane.

Soon afterwards, it became obvious to MacBean that she enjoyed his lavish lifestyle as much as he ever did. In fact, she enjoyed it more, much more. Expensive jewelry, a sports car, short vacations at two different islands, and expensive wardrobes, she wanted it all. But MacBean was so glad to be putting his key in the apartment lock knowing there was someone finally behind that door, he honestly didn't care about the expenditures, at least not at first.

Angela eventually started realizing how much money MacBean made, and when she compared that to her salary, her thought was to ask, "Why should I work? What's eighty thousand a year when my husband makes thirty million?" MacBean didn't understand her attitude because he knew that lawyers could also make small fortunes if they had the contacts, the kind she now had through MacBean. But she was having none of that. Then, and only then, did it dawn on MacBean that he should have listened to his own lawyer's advice and had Angela sign a prenuptial. His arrogance, thinking neither Angela nor his own feelings at the time of the marriage would ever change, could be costly.

Angela may have been more educated than his first two wives, but MacBean realized he was trapped yet again. Only this time, he wasn't as sure it was all his fault.

On Columbus Day weekend, the couple went to the Vineyard home. Angela mentioned that they should buy a larger home on the Vineyard. so they snapped up a mansion for two and a half million with a mortgage of one and a half million and selling the other home as the down payment. The Scotsman in MacBean was not only dead, but buried, deeply, deeply buried.

As he continued to work long hours, Angela began to spend more time at the Vineyard, hanging around with celebrities that lived part of the year on the island. Married less than one year, they managed to spend only a single full day together each week. Even that one day was filled with visiting or hosting Angela's new friends. MacBean was so exhausted from his work load that he tried to ignore the situation. An occasional walk on the beach on a Sunday morning was about the only quality time they spent together, in addition to sleeping together Saturday evenings when he arrived home.

As his career continued to blossom on the business side, his personal life deteriorated. He called Angela from different parts of the country on business trips because she never found the time to accompany him. MacBean was a financial networker of note, but Angela's social networking put him to shame. Some weekends MacBean did not even make it to the Vineyard due to international business trips or simply too much work to do at the office. Angela did not seem to mind, as long as she had her friends and MacBean's financial support. She collected Vineyard intelligentsia and pretty things at equally impressive rates. MacBean knew he was being used but continued to bury his anger in his work. When she would pretend to be lovey-dovey, especially when with friends, his anger only grew. But when they were alone and her true feelings for him became apparent, his anger became an overwhelming sadness with a good deal of self-pity thrown in. He wondered at times whether the age difference was playing a role. He even wondered why she couldn't just pretend to love him, since she obviously loved his money. At first, he felt empty inside, thinking that the only way he could have love was to buy it. Then he'd think back to Penelope and Brandy, and he realized he'd always tried to buy it. Here now was a third failure to prove the pattern.

MacBean's thirty million plus a year was simply not enough to support two people who substituted money for love. Outside of his two homes and his retirement portfolio, MacBean had no significant savings in spite of all the money he'd made. Saving was a thing of the past, as he and Angela seemed to be in a competition to see who could spend his money faster. At least business was doing well in 1985, and MacBean still continued to believe that low assets weren't of concern as long as his earning power remained high. In his mind, there was always plenty of time to save. When someone has the confidence to believe without any doubt that their career success would never end, saving for a rainy day could seem overly cautious.

October 19, 1987: The largest single day crash on Wall Street with $500 billion in losses. While not the precipitating factor, many credit the size of the losses to computer programs that automatically sold when specific prices were reached, thus selling off thousands of stocks; and the same program also prevented buying. This crash resulted in the implementation of protocols to override automated buying and selling. (18)

When the 1987 crash occurred, most of KBL's clients were impacted somewhere in the middle range, not small amounts but not enough to cause disaster. MacBean's brilliance had always been to make steady money without jeopardizing significant assets. But the crash was enough to temporarily slow down his and everyone else's earnings until confidence could be regained. This meant less spending was required by both Mr. and Mrs. MacBean. After two years of marriage, it was clear it was over. MacBean figured out that he had only spent a hundred days out of those two years with Angela. When he told Angela, she had a choice to spend less of his money and go to counseling together or divorce, she laughed. She claimed later it was because she thought he was kidding. But he knew the truth. To her, he was a complete fool. She said she would sue him for everything he had, that she would own him before it was all over. By the end of the process, MacBean knew she'd been right about all of it, including him playing the fool.

Angela got the penthouse in New York City, the house on the Vineyard, and part of his retirement portfolio, which was approximately two million dollars. The only good part was that he only had to pay her alimony for two years or when the Vineyard home was sold, whichever came first. Of course, he still had to pay the mortgages, but he did get to keep one luxury car. *Three marriages, three strikes, I'm out! No more marriage for me. Some people were just unlucky in love, and I was one of them.* A couple of years later, Angela would take MacBean to court and successfully get the rest of his retirement portfolio.

MacBean thanked God they had no children to support. Yet he wondered whether children might have been the glue to hold his marriage together. *No, I'd be just as lousy a father as I've been a husband.*

Shortly after the '87 crash and the divorce, MacBean bought himself a small, efficient house in a nice neighborhood, his parents' small house in fact, for a quarter of a million. He had let it go after his dad died, feeling he was too busy with other things. He used what cash he had left to avoid a mortgage. It was a place of comforting memories to go home to after a long work day. Coming back to his own old homestead brought back memories of Mum and Dad and the love they shared as a family. This helped MacBean ease his mind about the latest fiasco with Angela and the legal system. He remembered his lawyer telling him after the Brandy divorce, "Next time, MacBean, get a prenup for Christ sake". But MacBean was too vain to think he'd botch up yet another marriage! Being in his old house made him stop and wonder how his mum and dad had such a strong marriage without a lot of financial means.

One thing he had learned, from three failed marriages, was to be savvy enough to place the house in an irrevocable trust, with his attorney as the trustee, so no one could touch that most valued asset. With this trust, he could not have full control over the property but would have the right to reside there as long as he lived.

True to his belief in his earnings power, MacBean started to save money. Without Angela's spending or his own, he was quickly back up to about four million dollars, and he moved that into the trust also. This money was placed in dividend-paying stocks that yielded approximately one hundred eighty thousand a year. He used that for all the house-related expenses. He also made sure that someday a Catholic charity would benefit from the trust. He knew his parents would have been pleased with that. If the property was ever rented during his lifetime, the trust would receive the rental income, since expenses were the responsibility of the trust. It had been a long time since MacBean had given the same kind of thought and care he gave to a client's portfolio to his own personal finances. It had been a long time since he'd done something financially sensible on a personal level without blowing the money he had saved.

Coming up on forty-three and with 1990 only a couple months away, he convinced himself that this might be the last time he could rebound fully and still have time to rebuild assets and his retirement portfolio. Talking with a colleague MacBean had said he felt able now to focus on what mattered, his work. When the co-worker said back to him, "Do you know what you just said?" it was as though a thunderbolt had struck MacBean in his tracks. Three marriages totaling just a few years of his life, and yet he felt afraid of living the rest of his life without love. *I don't think I know what love actually is. I know it when I see it, I've seen it in fact, but I don't seem to be able to see it clearly enough to find it myself. It's like fog. I can see it, but I can't grasp it, it evaporates in my hand.* MacBean had never spent so much time thinking about his life, and he was beginning to feel growing pains that made him quite uncomfortable when he thought about doing what he needed to do and equally uncomfortable when he thought about not doing what he needed to do.

He began to work smarter, and that meant working fewer hours each day, even though he still loved the actual work. He also stopped spending as a means to demonstrate genuine success. The yacht, the club and the luxury cars were all gone. If he spent less, he didn't need to work as many hours. *How did I forget such a basic principle?*

He still made more than any superstar athlete and was grateful for that. Fortune, Forbes, and the Wall Street Journal plus other magazines were always writing about him. There wasn't a day that went by without seeing his name in some kind of paper or magazine. He'd even made the cover of Fortune a couple of times, including immediately after the '87 crash because the KBL clients had fared so much better than many others.

MacBean knew that he was a success in business but a personal failure. He didn't want his success to be a compartmentalized one. He wasn't sure how to do that, but he was determined to try and find out. He limited his work days to eleven hours a day and every Saturday for eight. For the most part, it worked. He enjoyed having a couple hours in the evening and some weekends to do what he wanted, such as taking a walk or relaxing at home. But still, something was missing. He would not allow himself to be totally at peace until he figured out what his definition of personal success should be.

His staff at KBL now had thirty-five hundred clients, and he was still in charge of Triton indirectly. Triton continued to be on top of the latest innovations involving the computer industry, and the company was still growing, demonstrating that the rewards of investing in top talent would also continue to pay off.

In February, 1993, the World Trade Center was attacked by terrorists with a truck bomb in the parking garage below the North Tower, intended to send the North tower crashing into South Tower. Although that plan failed, six people were killed, and over a thousand were injured. (19)

In spite of his wanting to build a personal life, MacBean still traveled extensively, logging over a hundred fifty- thousand miles a year, and some of the best clients at KBL throughout the world wanted to have meetings with him, personally. He might not be their direct broker on a daily basis, but he was still the man in charge. Thus, he was quite startled one morning, as he rose at 5 A.M., stopped for a coffee and bagel to take into the office, and saw an old couple sitting on a park bench feeding the pigeons. They touched each other affectionately, talked quietly, laughed at the silly birds, and when they rose, the man helped the woman to stand, and then the woman helped the man, as they slowly walked away while the birds took off in flight and scattered everywhere. It was then that MacBean realized he was no longer happy just being a successful broker. He didn't want to grow old and not have someone who cared enough about him to stick around when the time came that feeding pigeons with a loaf of stale bread from a park bench was the highlight of the day. *I'm an important man, but I'm not the most important man to a single other human being.*

MacBean decided that to find another woman it would have to be for what he was and not what he had. But he was beginning to understand that he had to be ready for it as well. He couldn't be a successful businessman, without first being a successful man. He just wasn't sure yet what that truly meant.

His first step was to stop worrying about achieving more financial power in the business arena than he'd already achieved. *I'm forty-five now and just now figuring this out?* After about the tenth time of wishing he could call Jack Slade, he decided he would do the next best thing and call Sam Slade. He was nervous about doing that since he'd neglected to call him since voting to strip him of his company's leadership. But he dialed the number anyway. *Do you want it to be like Bloomberg?* Sam answered, but MacBean didn't recognize the voice at first, it sounded so positive, upbeat, downright happy.

"Sam? Is that you?"

"MacBean? "

"Look, Sam, I know you might not want to talk to-"

Sam interrupted him. "You kidding me? Leaving the company was the best thing that ever could have happened to me."

"You don't have to say that for me."

"MacBean, you may be a very important man on Wall St., but believe you me, I wouldn't say that just for you".

"Oh, oh no, of course not. I just meant-"

"Stop your hemming and hawing, and tell me when you're gonna come visit me, you old son of a gun!"

MacBean visited Sam on his houseboat moored on a small marina on Long Island. Not a big fancy one with lots of yachts, but a smaller one that included fishing boats. The boat, itself, was immaculate but cozy. Sam's wife was visiting family in Ohio, and he seemed genuinely pleased to see MacBean. They talked for a solid four hours about Wall St. business and about each other. Sam had suffered a breakdown of sorts after losing the company helm, but he'd bounced back with a vengeance. But not on Wall St. Sam had taken his money and established a foundation called Jack's Place. The foundation helped to find housing for homeless veterans, including purchasing and rehabbing multiple family dwellings for veterans needing a little help getting back on their feet, for whatever the reason.

"MacBean, Jack's Place has given my life meaning, purpose. I would give my own life to have Jack among the living, but since I can't, helping people in his name helps me deal with the sadness. It's as if Jack's with me when I visit a veteran. Oh, I don't do any of the service providing, I'm not qualified for that. But I help scout out houses for potential rehabbing, and I get to meet some of the veterans living in those houses across this country. And I chair the foundation's investment committee. I still love making money, but for what it can accomplish for others, not what it can do for me."

By the time MacBean had left, Sam had gotten not only a donation to the Foundation from MacBean but had also extracted something else from him. "Once before, MacBean, I got you to make me a promise, to finish college, remember?" Sam said to follow him into the bedroom where there was a wall of photographs and memorabilia, including MacBean's college diploma from Manhattan College.

"I can't believe you kept that."

"Course I did. You were like another son to me. Maybe that's why it hurt so much when you didn't abstain from the vote."

"I'll never forgive myself for that, Sam".

"I'm not saying that to make you feel bad, son. I'm wanting to get another promise from you."

"What's that?"

"I want you to promise me that you will ask yourself every single morning from now until the day you die, what can I do today for somebody else that they can't do without my help? Will you do that, MacBean? For your old friend, Sam?"

"I'll try."

"HAH, that's just what you said back then. Remember what I said?"

"Don't try: do it!"

"Don't try, just do it! The kind of focus you put on making money, put that same focus on why you're making it."

MacBean left Sam and his houseboat that day, feeling he'd met that rare human who was genuinely happy in his life. He would try to honor Sam's wishes, but he didn't yet have the confidence that he would succeed. Later that night, he bolted upright in bed with the thought that Sam was what Bloomberg had meant by a "mensch".

MacBean began budgeting some of his savings to give to charities. And he began to notice people who seemed happy: a waiter at the club when he showed MacBean pictures of his family, which MacBean had asked to see, something he'd never done before; an elderly man at a lunch counter who volunteered to share his lunch with MacBean because he had only ordered a coffee, the richest man on Wall St. and an old man was going to skip half his lunch for him, and a young woman with a small child who asked her child to give the last of his ice cream cone to a hungry, stray dog. MacBean was still running KBL and involved at Triton, but his desire to work as hard as he had been was waning. And yet he hadn't actually done so yet. *What am I waiting for?*

All the money he'd wasted to this point in his life was a hard pill to swallow. But MacBean still believed he had learned from past mistakes. The fact that he had to keep saying that repeatedly had not yet dawned on him.

He started to trust his staff more and began to relinquish more of his duties. When he realized it was safe to pass responsibilities to others without worrying about it, it was a "wow" moment! It surprised him to think it came easier to him than he ever thought possible. He wished he had delegated more earlier in life, but better late than never. Sam Slade continued to be someone to emulate.

MacBean didn't voice it consciously, but he was setting the table to make one last effort at a long-term relationship, preparing himself for one more try. He had free time, now, or at least what passed as free time in his world.

***In 1996, the average cost of a new house was $118,200, and the average income annually was $36,300. A loaf of bread was $1.15, and the minimum wage was $5.15.* [20]**

One day, Sam was coming into the city on business and asked if MacBean had time to spend Saturday with him. When we met, I told Sam that I'd finally reached a point I was going to go after love again. Sam responded, "You don't go looking for love, love finds you. Right when you least expect it, it will happen." MacBean was hoping good old Sam was right.

It was December of 1996, and MacBean was turning the big five-o in a few days. He was in Rome visiting Alberto Rossolini, his wealthiest European client. On this trip, Rossolini wanted to combine business with pleasure. He asked MacBean to spend an Italian Christmas with his family. To his own surprise, MacBean accepted. The joy, love, and family bonding made MacBean feel the way his parents said they'd felt on their trip back to Scotland, although MacBean doubted the Scots could match the Italians hug for hug. They took MacBean into their Italian hearts and treated him like family. *This - this is what home is supposed to feel like, this is what I've been missing.*

MacBean and Rossolini went to a little restaurant together called La Cantina. Rossolini had found out from MacBean's staff that his birthday was on Christmas Eve. The Italian businessman had secretly hired a couple of professional musicians, a piano player and someone who played a beautiful mandolin. They were serenaded while sharing a delicious lunch. It was a complete surprise to MacBean, and yet it was a pleasurable experience that he would never forget. The musicians sang a stilted "Happy Birthday" to him in English. It was the best Christmas Eve and birthday he'd had since leaving his parents' home.

Yet the evening was much more than a birthday

celebration. When MacBean laid eyes on the beautiful hostess at this restaurant, with her olive complexion and a warm smile that gave him instant peace, he felt a rush like never before. His heart was pounding, and he would have sworn he could hear hers doing the same. But MacBean also knew this was the usual pattern he had for deciding," this is the woman for me" - before he actually got to know her. *Slow, go slow now; don't screw this up by moving too fast.* Over and over he repeated it.

MacBean asked Rossolini if he knew the woman. He told MacBean that she had been the hostess at this restaurant for about three years, and her name was Maria, and that's all he really knew. It was all the start MacBean needed. Maria did not speak any English, but that didn't matter. Rossolini noticed MacBean's infatuation with her, and he snuck into the kitchen to get her last name.

MacBean was set to go back to the US the day after Christmas, and he left a small note with his name and address for Maria, written in English, figuring someone could translate it for her. The note said that he would come back to Rome soon and would like to see her again. On the plane trip home, he couldn't take his mind off Maria, repeating *let love find me* every five minutes. The trip back home seemed much shorter due to his daydreaming. It was a very rare occasion for his mind to be completely off business. Rossolini had just given him over twenty million dollars to invest, but it was Maria that MacBean was thinking about. She mailed him a short note, written by someone in English, but signed by her. Her simple note said that she hoped he had enjoyed his holiday visit to Italy and to La Cantina.

Rossolini called MacBean a couple days later and told him that Maria's last name was Fontana and that she was definitely single and unattached. MacBean blushed a little thinking about the note he'd left her without even knowing if she were single. MacBean asked for the address of La Cantina and shortly thereafter sent a short letter to her attention at the restaurant.

He said he'd be back in Rome the end of January, even though he hadn't had such plans originally. But he was on a plane to Rome the last day of January 1997.

Once in Rome, he headed straight to La Cantina. Trusting to luck, he'd found Maria on duty. Maria was thirteen years younger than MacBean and never married. In fact, she still lived at home. Her padre, Angelo, wanted to know everything about MacBean. He'd spent the last month catching his daughter lost in daydreaming. Even without any formal dates with his daughter, Angelo was already wondering why a guy like MacBean would go back and forth across the Atlantic to see his daughter. The financial success that MacBean had achieved was of no concern to Angelo. What would concern him were three divorces by a man raised Catholic. It would be a hard sell to win this man's daughter. And with no family back in the US to help win Angelo over, and needing to essentially convince the entire Fontana clan, MacBean knew he was facing an uphill battle. He just kept telling himself that the slower it went, the more chance of real love finding him.

When MacBean invited Maria to come and visit him in New York City, it did not sit well with Angelo, who insisted that Maria's mum, Rosalina, accompany her. Needless to say, Maria and MacBean did not sleep together on that first visit. They needn't have worried so much because there would be no sleeping together on any other visits in fact, because Maria made it plain that even though it was the nineties, she still believed in saving herself for the man who would be her husband for life. What her edict provided was time for both of them to get to know each other, how they thought, how they felt, what they wanted from life. And MacBean realized this was one way that love would find him - by giving it the time it needed to have to develop into two people becoming friends as well as lovers.

Although both knew for months that marriage was in the future, it was not until MacBean finally asked her to marry him, that she was fully convinced he would be her one and only husband. She then softened her edict, but elicited from MacBean a promise never to let her parents know. "I'm a good Catholic girl, JoJo, but I'm no nun!". That was the first time she had called him "JoJo" instead of MacBean, and he loved it, he loved her more than he ever thought humanly possible. *Perhaps that was the point – it was only humanly possible to love like this.* It wasn't easy for either padre or mama to allow the marriage, but they knew Maria was as crazy about MacBean as he was about her. The Fontana's were humble people, Angelo was a potter by trade. They understood the concept of money, but not how one "makes" money by moving it around and around. "But what do you make, Mr. MacBean?" Angelo had asked. All MacBean could answer was, "I make rich people richer." *What a silly thing to say.* Angelo thought *what a silly thing to do.*

For the first time in his life when working, his mind started drifting toward Maria. Daydreaming was not something he'd ever experienced at work. MacBean was the man with the focus that kept KBL and himself at the top. He grew puzzled when he thought to himself *how did such a lovely woman like Maria stay single so long?* But he answered it quickly with *She's been waiting for me!*

It was now July 1997. Rossolini picked MacBean up at the Rome airport and dropped him off at his hotel, reminding him that he had guest quarters at his house if he preferred. MacBean thanked him for his kindness, smiled and told him he was here on a personal mission, and of course Rossolini knew exactly what MacBean meant. He told Rossolini that if there were any business to conduct, he would be available for him, but Rossolini replied that would not be necessary this trip, as the staff at KBL was taking good care of him. The Italian businessman smiled and wished MacBean luck.

Luck wasn't on MacBean's side that day. Arriving at the restaurant, he was told it was Maria's day off, and she was out shopping with friends. The trip was meant to be a surprise, and

Maria had switched her usual day off that week in order to join her friends. The twenty-four hours spent in his hotel would seem an eternity to MacBean.

He ended up going to Rossolini's office after all. He made some calls and reviewed the client's portfolio. It had increased substantially since the last time of review. The KBL investment staff was doing terrific work, and that pleased MacBean. He had taught his staff well, and they knew the value of a satisfied client as the best way to grow a firm.

Rossolini took it upon himself to call the owner of La Cantina to get Maria's phone number. Without MacBean knowing, he called and told her mama to tell Maria as soon as she returned home that MacBean was in town. Later that evening, Maria went to Rossolini's office and surprised MacBean. What a kind gesture for Rossolini to make. It reminded MacBean that he had not yet begun fulfilling his promise to Sam. *It wasn't even a big deal, just help with a language barrier, and without even being asked. I'll try harder, Sam.*

As time went by, Maria continued learning a few words of English and MacBean picked up a few words in Italian. They hadn't mastered each other's language, but it was more than enough for them to communicate pretty well. When they went to an Italian restaurant, they always found kind waiters who would listen to them and teach them a few more words of each other's language. Even though Maria worked during this trip to Rome, MacBean would go to her restaurant when she was ready to leave, and they'd stop for an expresso on the way home. She would talk about the people she seated that day and how some were so funny and others so sad and still others so happy. Talking in broken English, Maria pointed out everything about them. MacBean was astonished at the amount of information she could glean from simply looking at people, observing them ordering or eating. Occasionally, she would even make up stories that made MacBean laugh out loud. He would tell her stories of growing up and his business enterprises in the neighborhood that made Maria laugh. MacBean realized he told her little about his Wall Street life because there was so little joy in it to share. Those few minutes with her after her work shifts convinced MacBean that love had finally found him, and now that it had, he would never let it go.

MacBean extended his one-week trip to three weeks, the topic of much speculation around KBL, since such time away from the office for nonrelated business was unheard of. In that three-week period, Maria had only three full days off, and they spent virtually all of those three days together. MacBean always made sure that Maria was home by eleven those three nights. He was committed to earning her parent's trust. Every time he was with Maria, MacBean felt not just that his heart was beating faster than normal, but that it was in sync with hers, just like the first time. There were some moments when he wished he had met her fifteen years earlier, but he pushed those thoughts out by telling himself his usual "better late than never." He also had an inkling that the man fifteen years earlier was not the man of today. That man would not have patiently waited for love to find him. That man would not have treasured a simple cup of espresso with the woman he loved, as much as five-star dining at New York's most expensive restaurant.

MacBean explained to Maria about the career path he had taken and his three failed marriages. Maria seemed to understand, but it still did not matter to her. She thought that these past experiences made him a better man. MacBean was beginning to feel that way, too. She told him that as long as he made an honest living it did not matter how much he made. That was a pleasant sound to his ears. Maria also said that her padre was a hardworking man who made just enough to sustain them and that her mum lovingly accepted that. Her family had good old-fashioned values that MacBean thought had disappeared in today's world. He was starting to realize that his world was not the only world.

MacBean had reached the point of wanting to make it

official and move Maria back to the US, but knew her parents would not approve of that just yet. The last thing Maria wanted to do was hurt her parents, and he understood this perfectly even as he worried that his patience might not be boundless.

In late August MacBean returned to the US. He now called Maria every day to tell her he loved her and missed her. He planned on returning to Rome in six weeks, but having been absent for a while, the work had piled up, in spite of his excellent staff. He found it hard to believe he'd now been at KBL for thirty years.

It was mid-November before MacBean flew to Rome. As usual, Rossolini insisted on picking him up, and to his surprise, Maria was with him. Maria and MacBean hugged and kissed, and at her parents' request, she took him home to see them even before he could check into the hotel. They had found out more about his career and the three failed marriages, not the past of someone "good enough" for their daughter. Yet, Angelo could also see that Maria's eyes were filled with love. Her parents were definitely trying hard to accept her choice because of her happiness. Still, Angelo Fontana was an old-world padre. So, when he extended Maria's curfew to midnight for this trip, it was the Fontana's way of saying, "Your patience is paying off'. But the time went by too fast for them both, and this second good-bye was harder than their first.

Early in 1998, MacBean knew the time had finally arrived for both him and Angelo to make their decisions. He flew again to Rome and asked Angelo formally for permission to marry Maria. He knew he'd met a man who cared not a whit for MacBean's financial success beyond being able to put a roof over his daughter's head and food on the table. What he cared about was whether MacBean could make his daughter happy and be a good husband and a good father. It would require trust on the Fontana's part, but MacBean had earned some of that trust with his patient respect of the early courtship rules Maria's parents had established including visits to New York

City only if accompanied by Mama. The couple married in June of 1999, in Rome, MacBean fifty-two and Maria thirty-six. On MacBean's side of the wedding aisle were his senior staff, whose hard work during his absences had helped make the marriage possible. Sam Slade had been ill and could not be MacBean's best man, as he'd hoped. But Mr. Rossolini was also an excellent choice. Both the KBL staff and Mr. Rossolini knew Maria was right for MacBean and seemed truly happy for him.

The friends and relatives on Maria's side were beyond counting. At the wedding, he couldn't turn around without bumping into another cousin who bear-hugged and kissed him. When they left for their honeymoon, MacBean promised her parents that when they returned to New York City, he would make time for trips to Rome and for their visits to NYC.

When they arrived in NYC, they immediately prepared for what was to be a ten-day honeymoon in the Canadian Rockies. After that, they came back and settled down in their New York City residence. It felt strange to MacBean to be there with Maria without her mum.

Luckily, Rome was not a small city, so Maria adjusted to New York City quite easily. On MacBean's first night after work, he decided to take her to Little Italy. She loved it so much they began to go there for dinner weekly. Maria would talk to the staff in her native tongue and do the ordering for both of them. She also appreciated that MacBean was trying to help her feel at home. Their favorite spot was the least pretentious of them all, reminding them of their espresso dates.

Maria never complained when he worked ten or eleven hours a day or on a Saturday. She would meet him at the door, sit him down in a comfy chair, and give him a simple but effective shoulder rub. MacBean would never have believed how something so simple would come to mean the difference between a peaceful evening spent with not a thought given to business and the usual stress-filled night trying to predict tomorrow's market. Living in his parent's small home made

MacBean realize that there was more to happiness by being there with this woman than in living a materialistic lifestyle. Making money might make someone financially secure, but it also created a pressure that seemed impossible to lessen, no matter how much money was made. Now, a simple shoulder rub prompted a sigh of relief more satisfying than all the shouts of glee at making a killing on a stock exchange floor!

It was a simple life by two people who felt secure in their partner's unconditional love. MacBean made sure Maria called her family often and as much as she wanted to, and they already knew they were welcome at any time without notice. Even though MacBean now owned the house, he still considered it his parent's home, but he made sure Maria knew she could change anything about it that she wanted to. She changed just two things: she added a multi-burner gas stove for making her own Italian dishes with scratch sauce and a new four poster, king size bed, the kind she had always dreamed of having someday (having slept her whole life on a small daybed). Being a modest house, the bed literally took up the whole room. She had cried when she realized she hadn't bothered to measure, but MacBean told her the bed was a fitting symbol of their love -- filling every nook and cranny of their lives as the bed did the room. The bureaus were then ceremoniously moved to the other bedroom. MacBean only wished his parents could have met Maria. Oh, how they would have loved her! Being Catholic and planning on raising the children as such would have sent his mum right over the moon.

When he finally began working only ten hours a day, and just four hours on Saturday morning, MacBean felt he had managed to establish a satisfying personal life. He believed he was the happiest he'd ever been. Watching a TV show about Mt. Everest, MacBean declared "I don't need to climb Mt. Everest because I'm already at the top of the world!" To which Maria replied, "So where am I?" MacBean replied back, "Right next to me; don't you know you're my own Italian

Sherpa? Without you, I am lost."

MacBean had even reduced his business travel, and when he did travel, Maria usually went with him. She was genuinely interested in whatever locale they were in. She even took a part time job at Eduardo's Ristorante in Little Italy as a luncheon hostess, usually working three lunches a week. Not only did it keep her Italian fluent and her English credible but it also gave her time to expand her own culinary skills. Within six months, she was in the kitchen prepping food twice a week. "I am as happy as a clam -zuppa di clams!" she would tell people.

Having reduced his work load, and his salary from thirty to eighteen million, which allowed his staff to take on more responsibilities, life was getting better all the time: fewer business trips, more dinners at home, learning more Italian, and learning more about wines as Maria would sometimes get a gift of wine from the owner if she could tell the owner all about it, so she could in turn tell a customer. She was even considering going for sommelier certification down the road. MacBean encouraged all of her pursuits; it was delightful to see the joy she took in her life. Of course, it did take some persuasion on her part to get MacBean to agree to a bambino or two. He was over fifty, but Maria was impatient because of her age, as well. Yet MacBean could deny her nothing. They made the decision she would stop her pills and let nature take its course.

Evenings at home, MacBean would often tinker around on a computer he'd been assembling from components he'd purchased or salvaged from other computers. It had developed into a hobby he found himself enjoying more than ever. He would donate the rebuilt computers to churches and different charities. When he gave up his board positions, except for KBL, something he never imagined doing, he found he had the time to devote to his new hobby.

On Sundays, they sometimes took trips to the Smithsonian in D.C., the Jersey Shore, south coasts of Rhode Island and

Connecticut, wherever the spirit moved them to explore.

MacBean had brought up once that his mum used to pack his lunch when he still lived with his parents. A week later, Maria started packing him a lunch two or three times a week. She'd even found his old Superman lunchbox to put it in. Of course, he took a little ribbing for that. It was always healthy fare, such as spinach salads, fruits, yogurt, and sometimes even homemade biscuits. He treasured those lunches, he wasn't merely eating food, he was gaining sustenance.

One morning, MacBean called Maria right after leaving for work to ask about her own early morning assignment. She had begun to do some catering of small events for the restaurant, but she'd never done an early breakfast before. Her specialty was Italian dishes, but for breakfast? So, she perfected an amazing omelet with peppers, onions, pepperoni, and the most delicious Parmigiana Reggiano. She'd tried it out on MacBean and he wasn't lying when he said it was the most delicious omelet he'd ever tasted. When he called that morning, she was getting ready to leave for her friend's business in order to man the omelet station for a breakfast meeting. She was so excited to be a "real" chef. She told MacBean she'd be home by eleven that morning. As always, they ended with MacBean telling her he was still madly in love with her and she saying the same to him in Italian. Her event was at a financial firm on the sixty-eighth floor of the South Tower of the World Trade Center at 8 A.M. on September 11, 2001.

The morning of September 11, 2001 saw four terrorist attacks by al-Qaeda, with two of those attacks on the twin towers of the World Trade Center. Those attacks killed 2,977 and injured over 6,000 others. [(21)]

THE END OF THE BEGINNING

At 9 A.M., someone came into MacBean's office shouting, "We've been attacked!" MacBean went out to the conference room that everyone had crowded into to watch TV. He literally did not know what to do. He walked out of the office as if in a trance, and walked down to the World Trade Center, where chaos had erupted. He grabbed the arm of a fireman and screamed, "My wife is inside!"

The fireman yanked himself free, but gave MacBean a look of understanding and said, "We're doing our best, but you should get out of here now". A call came into MacBean's cell, but it was so noisy he couldn't hear. Then a text arrived. There had been a call for him saying the injured were being taken to area hospitals, but early casualties seemed to be at New York Downtown Hospital. There were no cabs available, so he started walking, running, walking, running in the general direction of the hospital. He arrived and walked in to ask about Maria MacBean, but it was too early for anyone to know anything specific. So MacBean sat and waited as if in a trance, until a woman came up to him at 1:00 AM and spoke to him in words he still couldn't process, then escorted him to a makeshift morgue where she lay still and lifeless underneath a sheet.

His life with Maria flashed before his eyes. His personal and business world collapsed around him. The hospital found a physician who could speak Italian, and he called Maria's parents to give them the bad news. MacBean sat in a hospital chair stunned and numb. He was told later that he screamed, "I should be the one, not her, I should be the one."

Two days later her remains were cremated and MacBean flew with her ashes to Rome via Canada for his last trip with her. There were so many people at her funeral, and his heart not only hurt for himself, but so deeply for her parents. Mrs. Fontana was able to speak to MacBean, but Angelo could say nothing. Maria's parents knew she was happy, and fortunately they did not blame MacBean, but he wasn't so sure about whether they blamed the U.S. He stayed with Maria's parents after the funeral for a few days. Angelo found the words "mia figlia" the next day. A few more words were added on the next. A few of the senior staff at KBL and Triton flew to Italy for the funeral to give their support. MacBean would not be able to recall the funeral in any detail later except for the unrelenting loss he felt, even to the point of questioning whether life would ever be worth living again.

When MacBean returned to work, he wasn't really there for the clientele. Some clients even started to complain about him, even though they recognized it was beyond his control. But clients were paying for his attention, attention he wasn't able to provide. His fifteen to eighteen million dollars a year did not matter anymore. He was fifty-four and on the verge of being washed up. Grief had swallowed MacBean whole.

As the world mourned, and some prepared to take action, MacBean only asked, *Why someone so good as Maria, why her? Why not me, for God's sake?* His anger became mixed with self-pity. He didn't blame God, but he couldn't understand how this had happened. *Why does evil win? How can anybody live a happy life knowing that at any time, it might end? How can I feel safe again – ever?* No, MacBean didn't blame God; he just wished He could do better. When MacBean dwelled on what had happened, he thought perhaps God was watching over him while he was establishing his career, and he had always felt that somehow God had reintroduced Sam Slade back into his life. But with Maria, he had finally thought God had forgiven him for mistakes made, and he'd been grateful for that. But there was now so much pain to endure he just knew it had to be a punishment of some kind; a living hell made just for JoJo MacBean.

The board of directors of KBL met without his knowledge and voted for a new president and CEO. Anyone could see that MacBean was not in his proper state of mind. Even MacBean knew that. His staff had their careers to continue, as did the rest of the employees at KBL. The company needed a new person to take the reins. *Now I know how it feels, Sam, I finally get it.* The company MacBean had taken from large and prosperous to the largest brokerage firm in both size and wealth in the U.S. and fifth in the world, was telling MacBean, "We don't want you". And once KBL was gone, Triton soon followed. The only upside was that it didn't seem important anymore, anyway. Nothing did, not even living.

He left KBL with a severance package of one and a half million dollars, netting him slightly less than a million dollars. A few told him to fight for more, but MacBean had no fight left in either body or soul. Adding insult to injury, Angela had found out. through the newspapers and from her inner circle, about his severance package. MacBean had already paid off her two mortgages by taking him to court, and she had drained his retirement account soon after the divorce. MacBean was so defeated he had no stomach for fighting with her. He gave her everything but forty-five thousand dollars which remained in his name. He sold the last two cars to eliminate the car loans. At least the trust could not be touched. There was enough income generated by the trust to cover the home expenses, with a little left for MacBean, at least for this MacBean.

He felt washed up, an old man in spirit if not in years. Drowning in self-pity, his depression was now complete. He kept telling himself how lucky he was to have a house to live in. And living on such limited means felt to him just what he deserved. He did not dwell on the fact that others would, indeed, find those limited means a rather lenient punishment.

Before taking his final leave of KBL, MacBean did something out of character, for usually he balanced himself carefully, brilliantly, on that thin line between things a little sketchy and outright fraud. That last day he lost his balance and fell over that line, taking along with him a list of his KBL clients. The list included information that had phone numbers and addresses and net worth of the thirty-five hundred clients that had been under his watch. He didn't know why he'd done it, perhaps to ask a few for help someday in the future, if his future included brokering. *Perhaps I'll end up doing something else. Maybe something less stressful, less responsibility. Once people know I've landed somewhere, they'll follow MacBean. Or perhaps I'll end up doing nothing at all.*

One morning, about four weeks after he was fired, MacBean had a bona fide nervous breakdown when he was found walking down the streets naked and crying. He was hospitalized for approximately three months, having gotten so drunk the night before wondering how he could live the rest of his life without Maria. He blamed himself for ever bringing her to the US. *Maybe if I had married her but stayed with her in Italy, this would not have happened.* Sam Slade sent him a nice letter explaining that his own illness of Parkinson's was keeping him homebound, but that MacBean should call him anytime night or day. Only one person visited MacBean. Not from KBL nor from Triton, but a Columbia professor stepped through his door.

"So, I see you're still carrying around that giant knapsack. Must be getting awfully heavy by now."

"What?"

"So much self-pity in it, it's a wonder you haven't drowned in it. Stinks, too, kind of like manure."

"You sure know how to cheer up a fellow, Rivers."

"I told you once to go fuck yourself and once to go find

yourself. I don't think you've done either, have you?"

"I married a woman I loved more than life itself. And she was killed by those Muslim bastards."

"Like almost three thousand others. Not saying it's not a tragedy. It is. But it's not just MacBean's tragedy. Remember that."

"You think it's easy, do you?"

"No, I don't. I think it's necessary, to remember I mean. And your wife would say it to you if you'd be still long enough to hear her."

"Don't you dare talk about my wife, you didn't even know her."

"Oh, but I did know you. I heard the gossip around Bloomberg's."

"You still go there?"

"Can't get a decent celery soda anyplace else."

"Why are you here, anyway?"

"What, you waiting for somebody else? Did I miss the line of people waiting to see the great MacBean? No?"

"Go away; just go away".

"You still haven't found yourself. Get away, see some of this country, see some other people besides clients, talk to them, listen to them. GO FIND YOURSELF." And with that Rivers walked toward the door.

"You mean like be a hobo?"

"There are no more hobos. You'd know that if you knew anything beyond Wall Street. There aren't any more open railroad cars. Hobos are now just homeless people."

"If somebody chooses to roam the country, then they're a hobo, not homeless. My dad used to tell me stories about hobos riding the rails."

"Have it your way. Go be a hobo. But for God's sake, go find out who MacBean is."

Once MacBean left the hospital, he passed time going to dumps and business dumpsters in the neighborhood to see if there were any old computers and spare parts not being used. He would assemble these makeshift computers on the days that he was mentally capable of doing so. It killed part of his time, but not enough of it. The severe pain was still there. He barely slept, and he was losing weight. But he also managed to sell a few of these computers to people in the neighborhood. His hobby, at least, kept him functional on some level.

In reality, he knew now he would never work in the same capacity as before. Not only did he not have the energy anymore, he had neither the desire nor the drive. A nervous breakdown doesn't exactly boost a man's confidence.

MacBean was a washed-up middle-aged businessman. He thought about all the money he'd made, and wasted, and that made him more depressed. He didn't mind dwelling on that, didn't mind dwelling on his failed marriages, didn't mind dwelling on Bloomberg, didn't mind dwelling on anything he'd ever done, as long as he didn't have to dwell on losing Maria. MacBean was literally driving himself crazy.

The drinking that had stopped after he'd met Maria, now began again with a vengeance, in effect taking him from workaholic to alcoholic. When not working on assembling computers from the used parts for the spare change, he was spending that spare change on drinks at a corner bar in the neighborhood called Sparkie's. A good day selling meant a little food to go with the cheap beer. He doubted he would ever drink wine again.

His typical day was two or three hours gathering old computers and computer parts and working on assembling them. The rest of the day he'd be down at Sparkie's drinking. Usually he'd arrive back home by 4 P.M., take a nap, sober up, and work a couple more hours assembling computers. By spending only the money he made on the computers, he was able to protect most of the forty-five thousand left in his severance package and the small amounts leftover each day after Sparkie's. In the back of his mind he could hear Sam's voice asking him about the promise he had made. *What could I possibly do for anybody, Sam?! Look at me now!*

Every evening on his way home from the bar, MacBean would ask *How could I go from dealing with smart influential business acquaintances and clients to hanging around with drunks who can't carry on a conversation about either computers or the market?*

Most of the time MacBean drank alone, sitting at the end of the bar, wanting no company. His life was a blur. He vaguely remembered thinking once before that his life was like the scene outside as seen from inside a speeding train. *Had it always been like that, or were there just times when I didn't bother looking out the train window?*

Many of the times he went to Sparkies, he would encounter a bartender that had known Lonnie, a burly Dutchman with a long white beard named Daan Klein but everyone just called him Claus. Each time MacBean came in, the bartender attempted to enter into conversation with him, but MacBean had no interest. Claus was a patient man who, bit by bit by bit, was wearing down MacBean's embarrassment at meeting someone who knew his dad. Finally, after about the tenth visit, Claus stopped treating MacBean with kid gloves and yelled at him outright. "Enough, fella, show some respect to your elders, and to your dad Lonnie, may he rest in peace!"

At that, MacBean burst out crying and ran from the bar. Claus was sure he'd driven the man from Sparkie's forever, but the next afternoon, MacBean returned.

He approached Claus at the bar. "I'm sorry, sir, for being rude to one of my father's acquaintances".

"Apology accepted. Take this drink, go sit over at that table in the corner, and I'll join you in ten minutes when my shift is over." MacBean walked with his drink to the table and sat.

From the bar Claus shouted "And don't drink it all by the time I get there. You're not getting another!"

Claus and MacBean sat and talked for three hours, with Claus nursing a club soda and MacBean his whiskey and soda.

By the end of their evening together, MacBean had promised the bartender that he would take his first step to sobriety by not coming to Sparkie's again. Claus told MacBean about his own struggle with alcohol, and how a good man named Lonnie MacDyer had sat him down and spent an evening talking about life's disappointments, and how sometimes a person just has to say out loud to someone he respects, someone he doesn't want to disappoint, "I will try my best, and I'll start right now."

Claus told MacBean that night that even though Claus wasn't someone MacBean necessarily respected, since he didn't really know him, that MacBean should think of Claus as if he were Lonnie. "Lonnie saved my life, so I think, in a way, he is a part of me now and forever. You disappoint me, son, it's the same as disappointing your dad."

MacBean, not wanting to disappoint but to honor his dad's memory, stopped drinking and began to gain a little of his positive thinking back. He knew he did not miss the stress of his business career. As much as he loved business, he couldn't handle the pressure of working at that pace anymore. If he started up again, he would probably kill himself going into overdrive because of his workaholic tendencies. Not a young man anymore, MacBean knew those days were now over physically, emotionally, psychologically, in every way possible.

He had never stopped reading business periodicals and newspapers that he found in trash cans and bus stops and on an occasional visit to a library. MacBean couldn't resist keeping up with stock market activity and the related current events. But now he found himself reading, not from boredom, so much as wondering how he might make a living with his expertise but without eighty-hour weeks and killer stress. He could control his drinking until he found himself bored by staring at the four walls, which would in turn precipitate a binge episode. On those times, he always managed to call Claus and express his shame. Claus would say, "Tell shame to go to hell. Your dad understands you are trying. Lonnie was a patient man. Patient doesn't mean forever, but it can wait as long as you're not giving up."

He wasn't sleeping well because he kept thinking about where his future was headed and whether he even wanted a future. He sold his expensive, hand- tailored suits to a second hand clothing store for pennies on the dollar. It sickened him to even think about dressing the part of the successful businessman. He said his goodbye to Claus and promised him that he would never give in again. Claus knew from his own such promises that it might not be true, but he knew MacBean meant it with every fiber of his being to be his truth.

A hobo is defined as someone traveling from place to place looking for work. Pre-World War II, most hobos rode in open rail cars or on top of them.[22] ***Hobos held an International Convention of Hobos in 1927 in Minneapolis.***[23]

By the sixties, most trains no longer had open cars, and hoboes by that definition had all but disappeared by 2002. The homeless, however, had not.

It was New Year's Day of 2002, at the age of fifty-five, and with forty-three thousand still left in his bank account, when MacBean concluded it was time to pack a few clothes into a backpack *(a real one, thank-you very much, Rivers Fitzpatrick)* along with his ATM card and his old KBL client list. He knew his needs were few: clean clothes, a decent meal now and then, a safe place to sleep occasionally, and a way to travel from town to town. He figured he could repair a few computers for small businesses and sell computers he'd rebuilt from salvaged parts.

This would allow him to hit the ATM less frequently. He also thought he might be able to give stock tips to the restaurant and deli owners in exchange for an occasional meal. He could continue to find reading materials discarded by others, as well as use libraries. MacBean's confidence was beginning to break through his fog of depression. He knew he had the smarts to get by just as he'd done in high school with those successful side businesses. But how to travel still eluded him. He wished he could live the full hobo life, jumping on and off trains. *What's the equivalent to a hobo life? Is there any other way I can ride the rails?* After a trip to Penn Station, MacBean realized that one more investment in this new life could provide travel and a safe place to sleep from time to time. He purchased an Amtrak Rail pass that gave him unlimited access to Amtrak, any train at any time for a year. MacBean figured he could find a way to make enough money to buy another pass as each year presented itself. And if he took an overnight train, he'd get some good sleep, while interspersing it with less sound sleeping on the road. *Life on the road, no responsibilities, no expectations, no pressure, just relying on my own wits.* He now had a plan, something to hold onto, something to keep back the dark thoughts of calling it quits on life. The only thing still keeping him awake nights was whether he could control his drinking. But he knew the only way to find that out would be to do it. He smiled as he thought about Sam Slade's twice telling him, "Don't think about it, do it!" MacBean wished he had the nerve to call Sam, but he was embarrassed for Sam to see how far he had fallen and to also realize MacBean was not yet following his second promise made to Sam. Instead, the night before he left, he wrote to Sam, asking forgiveness for being a failure and thanking him for everything that he'd done for MacBean. He also wrote to Rivers, thanking her for telling him to "find yourself". Without telling himself those two words over and over, MacBean wasn't sure he'd be leaving on a train in the early morning. He dug out his parents' old Polaroid, with an unopened film cartridge luckily, and snapped a picture of his backpack, writing on it "my stinky backpack" and enclosed it with his letter to Rivers.

MacBean had worried about leaving his parents' home. He was relieved when he found a renter at two thousand four hundred a month, which went into the trust that held the real estate, with the income from that trust now more than offsetting the expenses. On New Year's Eve, 2002, JoJo MacBean finally felt ready to hit the open road. He hitched a ride to Glastonbury, Connecticut. There'd be plenty of time for the train later. He wanted to feel the wind, feel the freedom, feel himself coming back to life.

When we are flat on our backs, there is no way to look but up. – Roger Babson

4

LIVING THE "HOBO" LIFE

2003 – 2005

The market began 2003 at 8607 and ended 2005 at 10717.

Glastonbury was a rather affluent small town. MacBean slept in the park or small alleys, or sometimes in vacant buildings, especially if the nights were cool, as they could be in spring and fall, although he'd stuffed a wool blanket into his backpack. Occasionally, he would spend for a light meal. Otherwise, he would watch people on the street closely to see what they might deposit into a trash can, so he might retrieve it while it was still fresh. He was, in fact, astounded at the food people routinely wasted. The town had little crime, and there were few visibly homeless people. MacBean's adjustment to life on the road was relatively quick under these ideal circumstances for a novice hobo.

He located a deli in town called Melke's. He offered the owner help with his new computer system in exchange for a daily free meal. The system did have a couple glitches that MacBean was able to resolve, but mostly it was the "show me, don't tell me" instruction the deli owner needed, which the computer installation company didn't have the patience for. The owner had originally thought he was doing a good deed, but realized quickly on that he'd gotten more than his value of the meals back. With the killing the owner made on the stock tip recommendations from MacBean, the owner offered to add some cash to the bargain. But MacBean suggested that the only additional thing he needed was a place to wash up every day and the use of the laundry room. It wasn't long before MacBean became the best-groomed homeless guy on the planet. Even though the computer project only took two months, the owner eventually trusted MacBean so much that he let him sleep in a cot in the back room on the bad weather nights even after the owner had mastered the computer system.

By the time spring rolled around, he could take a bath on warmer weather days in a small pond nearby. He bought a couple outfits at a local Salvation Army store. In the six or seven months he was in Glastonbury, he'd only spent about five hundred out of pocket, what he used to spend in five minutes. MacBean was getting by very well without any pressure and with no problem saying no to alcohol. But by June, he realized he was too comfortable. Life on the road couldn't be so comfortable as to lull him into a sense of complacency. *I'm not going to find myself by planting myself the first place I land, no matter how safe it feels. And there's nobody here to tell my story to.* Until that moment, he hadn't even realized he wanted to share his past with anyone. Now he believed that a big part of finding himself meant sharing his life story with others who might benefit from hearing it. He hitched a ride with a trucker and made his next stop that summer of 2004 in the nearby town of Somers, another very nice, very affluent town. After two days, he'd had enough of Connecticut. *I've got to get out of here, head someplace I don't feel so at home or so safe.* The next morning, he was on a train headed to Montana, still unsure of what town he wanted to settle on as his first stop. He had donned a wrinkled, but clean, Polo shirt and wrinkled, but clean khakis for the train ride. He couldn't help but hear his mother's voice admonishing him if he wasn't looking his best for a train ride. He just hoped she'd understand the wrinkles.

He was in awe of the beauty of the state. It made him feel both infinitesimal and yet part of something bigger than himself, similar to how he felt seeing the Rockies with Maria. And he smiled at the memory, realizing perhaps for the first time, *yes, I can remember some things now with a smile instead of pain. Thank you, God.* He couldn't remember the last time he had thanked the Man.

He got off the train in Missoula because he'd asked someone if Montana had any homeless population. The person he'd asked had assumed that MacBean was asking because he didn't want to be around the homeless. But, of course, MacBean's question was in order to find the "hobos" he would share his story with. After exiting the train, he went into the station and carefully took off and rolled up his khakis' and shirt and put them into the backpack as carefully as he could, then donned an old pair of jeans and a tee.

He left the station and started to walk towards the downtown. When he reached it, he first found the public library and then looked for any underpasses or bridges, places frequented by homeless. It was clear Montana didn't have many homeless. Then again, it didn't have many people! But MacBean was determined. He walked to a nearby park and sat on a bench. A few minutes later, a young man sat down next to him and asked if he wanted to buy something.

"Something? What's something mean?"

"You know. . something. Umm, weed, maybe?"

"Oohhhh, drugs. No, my drug is alcohol. Sorry."

"Hey, no problem. I never seen you here before, have I?"

"No, I'm from, well, it doesn't matter. "

"You need a place to crash tonight?"

"Sure. You know someplace?"

"Follow me. Not too close though."

"Uh, OK". With that, MacBean followed the young man about three feet behind him, for reasons he couldn't even guess at. After a fifteen-minute walk, the two men were in a small wooded section of the park, near a river. There were three other men there.

"Who you?" one of the men asked.

"MacBean".

"What the hell kind of name is that?"

"Mine". MacBean began to grow nervous about whether he should have trusted the young man.

"Christ sake, relax, we're not gonna do anything. It's clear you're new to this. What are you, a narc? Naw, you're too nervous right now to be a narc. A social worker, right? A do gooder come to save us!"

"Far from it. … Just a guy from New York. Maybe a guy with a story to tell, I don't know."

"What's that mean?"

"It's almost dark; you guys got anything to eat?"

"If you think we're gonna share with somebody who just got here, think again."

"Not what I meant. Meant I got a credit for a pizza at the place I passed on the way here. Anybody want pizza?" The young man knew MacBean hadn't stopped anywhere, but he decided to give MacBean the benefit of the doubt, if it might mean some pizza tonight.

The men stared at MacBean with a mixture of disdain, confusion, and hunger. MacBean took their stares to mean they would indeed like pizza.

Looking at the young man who had escorted him, he said, "Come on with me. We'll be back in a half hour."

"Hey, big shot, bring something to drink, too."

"Soda, got it."

"I don't mean soda, asshole."

"It's soda or nothing."

MacBean and the young man walked back towards town.

"You really got a credit at that pizza store?"

"No, but I got a little bit of cash with me. I'm trusting you not to let any of the others know that. I may be new to this, but I know enough not to let anybody know I got cash on me. I can trust you, right?"

"Yeah, sure. As long as you feed me, I'm yours, man!" With that the young kid laughed and smiled at MacBean. "Name's Jesús."

"MacBean". As Jesús extended his hand to MacBean, "Pleased to meet you, Jesús."

Loaded up with pizza and soda cans, the two men made their way back to the group, which had increased by two more men, just as Jesús had said it would.

Somebody had made a small firepit and the group sat around in silence eating and drinking as if it might be their last decent meal. MacBean looked at the group. *For these guys, any meal might be their last.*

Jesús asked, "So, where are you from anyway?"

Another man said, "And how the hell'd you get here?"

Where do I begin? He had no answer, and so he just began to speak, hoping his words would make a cohesive story of some kind. "I was little when I was born, stayed little until high school. I was christened Joseph Joshua MacDyer, Scottish you see. When I was about three, our priest said to my parents, 'He's no bigger'n a jelly bean.' I told him that I'm not a jelly bean, I'm a human bean. And Father, said 'That makes you a human MacBean.' And everybody from that day forward, except my parents, called me MacBean."

"And are you?" asked Jesús

"Am I what?"

"A human MacBean?" asked another one of the men.

"Well, I'm a MacBean, and I'm human."

"But are the two together something else?" asked the same man. He was quite old, with a short white beard and only a few teeth left from what one could tell.

"I, I, don't know what you mean," MacBean replied with a look of confusion.

"I can see you don't. Tis a shame you see. I'm Scottish myself. And I think your priest meant more than just to be funny. That would be for the Irish." The man snickered at his joke.

The men started to drift off to find a tree to lean against and sleep, or off on nighttime rounds of the trash cans for redeemable bottles and breakfast later. MacBean sat there and pondered where he might spend the night when the old man came up to him and said, "You're welcome to come with me, I've got a special place for the night." MacBean shook his head in agreement, and the old man led him to a small bridge over a dry bed and under that they both leaned against the concrete and fell asleep. When MacBean woke up, the old man was gone, but Jesús was walking towards him.

"MacBean, I'm going over to the food kitchen. Wanna come?"

"Where do you think the old man went to?"

"Oh, he gets up early to head over to the liquor store on South Park St. Sometimes, if he's lucky, there's a nip or two in the dumpster that accidentally didn't get emptied out of a box. Doesn't happen often, but, hey, you know how it is, with alkies, any chance is worth it."

"He's an alcoholic?"

"I never seen him drunk, but he sure can drink. So, who's to say?"

When they reached the food kitchen, MacBean was surprised not to find any of the other men he'd met last night. It was mostly women with their children, and a few other men scattered through. They had to listen to someone give a talk about God loving them all before they could eat. MacBean didn't mind, but then again, he wondered whether he would if he had to hear it every morning. But he found little joy in the group, not in the mothers or children, and not in those making and serving up the food. *Something is wrong here.* Later that evening, around the fire pit, Jesús told him that the homeless didn't like going to the food kitchen, so only the mothers, who had no choice for feeding their children, went on any kind of regular basis. "It wasn't the God stuff, it's the people who say they're godly, and then don't crack a smile the whole time they're there. The children sometimes laugh, but nobody else. It's like we're not allowed to have a single drop of happiness as long as we're eating their food."

"Why do you suppose they're like that? There has to be a reason. People aren't born unkind," said MacBean.

"I think it's the guy who runs the place. He's an unhappy man, so he don't want anybody else to ever be happy. Name of Dan DeVine."

"Maybe I'll pay a visit to Mr. DeVine."

"Don't go rocking the boat, MacBean."

The next morning, MacBean dressed in his khakis and Polo shirt, went down to the food kitchen. He asked if Mr. DeVine was around. He was shown into the back room with large cans of food items, reminding him of Bloomberg's store room.

When DeVine entered, MacBean offered his hand which DeVine shook. "Can I help you, brother?"

"Yes, Mr. DeVine. My name is JoJo" he hesitated "MacDyer of MacDyer, Bloomberg, and Slade." I'm the law office that's been retained by..."

"Don't tell me. I already know."

"You do? I mean, of course you do." MacBean had no idea what DeVine was talking about but knew enough to go with the flow.

"I knew sooner or later they'd catch up with me. How'd you ever find me?"

"We have our ways. It wasn't hard. Pretty obvious. How do you think?"

"My sister, of course. What happens next? Prison? Probation? What?"

"Well, I think..." MacBean tried to think what in the world DeVine had done, and what the consequences should be. *Think, MacBean.* "We've decided the very best outcome would be just to ask you to leave the state of Montana and never work again in a food kitchen anywhere in the U.S. If you agree to that, we won't bother pressing charges. After all, we're Christian folk, and we don't want to be too punitive. Our goal is just to get you to stop. . . uh…to stop. . ."

"I won't never pretend I know how to run a food kitchen again. Or how to save souls."

"Congratulations Mr. DeVine. Now. . .go?"

With that DeVine took off his apron, handed his pocket Bible to MacBean, and exited by the back-storeroom door. MacBean stood there trying to figure out how exactly this had happened. He then tied on the apron, put the Bible in the apron front pocket, walked out to the serving line and began serving up the powdered eggs and biscuits, with every other server staring at him but too afraid to ask what happened to Mr. DeVine. During the serving, MacBean told a few jokes, but nobody laughed. The next morning, instead of some fire and brimstone service, the diners heard MacBean tell a story. He spoke briefly about how he had once had a close friend whom he ignored until it was too late for that friend to even still know him. And how none of us should be too busy for the friends who love us. Then during his serving up eggs and biscuits, he told some jokes, and a few people laughed. By the end of the week, everybody was telling jokes and everybody was laughing. He was pretty sure Sam was somewhere smiling. That evening, MacBean decided he was ready to tell his Montana hobos who he really was.

"My name is JoJo MacBean, you ever heard of the famous MacBean of Wall Street, one of the richest men in America?"

Most of the men shook their heads. "Should we?" asked Jesús?

"No, I guess it wouldn't really matter to you."

"I know" said the old man with the white beard. "You're famous for being a bigshot at a really young age. And your wife died or something, right?"

"I never did get your name."

"Got no name, like God in the Old Testament."

MacBean was struck dumb at how similar a remark Bloomberg had once made to him when a ten-year-old MacBean had asked him how Bloomberg's God was different from MacBean's. "It's the same God, son, they're ALL the same God no matter what they're called. But at first the Jews' God had no name, so they called him Yahweh, a name too sacred to be said aloud."

"Are you OK? You look pale as a ghost. Didn't say I was God, said I just don't got a name."

"What do people call you?" At that, the group laughed since they all knew that the old man never told anyone his name.

"Nobody but a damned fool calls me anything."

"That pretty much means I have to call you something!" Again, the group laughed and waited for the old man to answer back. But the old man just stared at MacBean, then stood up.

"My name is Sol Golding." Sol offered his hand to MacBean, and the two shook hands.

"Thank you, Sol. Had a good friend once named Sol. I forgot about our friendship until it was too late. He was a great man who always gave me good advice."

"I know. You told that story at the food kitchen."

"How'd you know that? I didn't see you there."

"I wasn't, I heard about it. We all did. Some of us are thinking we might go back there once in a while now that you cleared up their case of holier than thou-ism."

MacBean felt embarrassed that the group had heard about his food kitchen exploits. He hadn't really done anything but stumble his way into getting DeVine to leave. Late that night, as he and Sol sat together in the old man's concrete hideaway,

MacBean asked him how he'd become homeless. Sol replied that when his son had gotten sick, he went into debt with medical bills. Then he'd started drinking heavily. When his son died, his wife left him to return back to her parent's house. But he kept on drinking until he found himself with no place to live except the streets. He stopped drinking once, but it didn't take. His second attempt was more successful, sober for two years while he worked as a stock clerk in a grocery store. Then the news of his ex-wife's death reached him, and his regrets became too much for sobriety to handle. "That's when I just gave up, son. I expected to be dead by now. Don't know why I'm not."

"Maybe you were waiting for me. Oh, no, that doesn't sound the way I meant it to. I didn't mean..."

Sol was laughing so hard he was rolling on the ground, and soon MacBean found himself rolling as well, until the two of them were so exhausted they fell asleep clutching their bellies from laughing so hard.

In the morning, Sol was gone, per his usual practice. MacBean got up and since he'd slept rather late and was famished, he decided to again treat the guys to pizza. He met Jesús on his way to get them.

"MacBean, did you hear?"

"Hear what?"

"MacBean…MacBean."

MacBean felt a wave of fear wash over him. "Just say it, say it fast, it helps sometimes."

"The old man, Sol, they found him dead this morning."

"Oh, sweet Jesús, I feel awful."

"I know, poor old guy."

"No, I mean, I maybe caused it. But that sounds . ."

"What are you talking about?"

"I said something to him last night, something dumb, but I didn't mean it to be. Maybe, no, never mind, I'm really being stupid. How'd he die, do they know?"

"Nobody knows yet for sure. But the story is weird, really weird."

"Tell me."

"They found him out in the woods, at this little altar he'd apparently built out of stone and sticks and shit. They say it looked like he was kneeling and had fallen over. And he was smiling, MacBean. Joe found him and said he had a grin on his face like he was laughing about something before he fell over.

MacBean began to cry before he knew he was even doing so. He immediately walked to the police station and asked where Sol's body had been sent. He then walked to that funeral home, stopping at the library to change into khakis and Polo. At the home, he found that Sol was to be cremated later that day with no one to notify and no one to give the ashes to. MacBean asked if he would be allowed to have the ashes. And then he told a lie to get them. "I'm his son, you see. I only found him here a few days ago, so you wouldn't know my name and address. We've been looking for him for several years. Please let me have them. Oh, I can pay, too. I don't have much, but I do have something. With that, he gave the funeral home the expensive watch he'd sewn into the hem of his old jeans for an emergency. The next day MacBean walked out of Davis Funeral Home with a small, simple urn filled with Sol Golding. He asked the other guys what they thought would be best for the ashes, and it was agreed that they would bury the ashes at the makeshift altar, and they would make a marker for it, and MacBean should keep the urn so somebody would remember the old man.

That night, MacBean began, "I'm leaving in the morning. It's time for me to move on. I'm trying to see some of this country, and maybe learn something. But I want to tell you more of my story before I go. For anybody who wants to listen."

All of the men gathered around the fire pit to listen. MacBean had popped again for pizza, and they would regret losing out on that again after tonight. But to a man they understood that MacBean somehow felt responsible for the old man's death, even though they had no idea why. People with trouble understand what trouble feels like.

"I need to tell you more of my story. I was once a very rich man. I mean I made millions."

"No way, man" came shouts.

"I went to Harvard, only for two years. I dropped out because I thought I could make more money on Wall Street. And I was right about that. But I was never good at love, or girls, you know? Never really had much luck."

"Are you kidding, with all that dough? You musta been doing something wrong!"

"You got that right. I was doing something wrong. I was using money to judge my success. I mean only money. Though I also admit that when I was at Harvard, that was a pretty good lady magnet, too. I been married four times."

"Divorced four times I bet!"

"NO, only divorced three times!"

"Oh shit, I was only kidding. You mean it, three divorces?!" The group was roaring in laughter at that.

"Three strikes and you're out, MacBean!" shouted someone.

"Three strikes because I didn't learn a goddamn thing from any of the three marriages. I just kept making the same mistake over and over and over."

"You mean you married the wrong woman over and over and over."

"Exactly. Only I didn't know it at the time."

"Slow learner is all!"

"All my money and still a slow learner when it came to something so important. I could make all the money in the world – and I did – but when it mattered, it meant nothing."

"Don't be so hard on yourself. It wasn't the money's fault, it was yours!" The group roared at that. And MacBean was struck with the brilliance of a remark made by a young, homeless man in Missoula, Montana named Jesús.

When he boarded the train the next morning, he was ultimately headed for Joplin, Missouri, only because one of the guys had suggested it as a relatively friendly place for homeless guys. Of course, the man hadn't been there in over ten years, but he remembered it as a fairly kind place. That meant the police didn't hassle you too badly. Besides, MacBean figured that Missouri sounded like Missoula, and that had to be a good sign, too. *It's as good a way to pick a town as any.* Before he boarded, Jesús handed him a small cross he'd made from two sticks and some string he'd found.

"It's to remember us by, MacBean. You can't make much else from sticks, so. . .anyway, what's better than to get a cross from Jesús himself?"

"Thanks, I'll treasure it; I mean that. You guys will always be my first hobo group."

"Now you watch out, OK? Homeless guys in some of the bigger places might not be so welcoming. I mean it, MacBean. You got lucky here. They're not all like Missoula."

"I got luckier than I had a right to be." With that, he gave Jesús a bear hug that the young man would not soon forget, like the ones Lonnie had always given his son. MacBean sat down in the train seat and clutched his small wooden cross while he slept. When he awoke, he put the cross next to the urn in his backpack where they would spend most of his journey.

PROPHETS OF JOPLIN

MacBean stepped off the train into the sweltering heat of an unusual February warm front in Joplin. He knew the bridge he was walking toward, as the Missoula guy had told MacBean about it. "Hey there" he shouted to the group sitting in the cool shade under the bridge. It was so hot MacBean wouldn't have been surprised to see a crowd of non-homeless taking advantage of the concrete coolness. Then he noticed that one of the men sat on the ground with two crutches next to him. The man's left pants leg was clearly empty.

"Hey there yourself. Who the hell are you?" shouted someone.

"Name's MacBean, came from Missoula. Guy up there named Joe Pantone said Joplin was a welcoming place. Was he wrong?"

"Could be, stranger. I never heard of Joe Pantaloon. Any of you?"

"I knew a Joe Panacotta once, guy was a real prick."

"Pantone. He's OK."

"Don't mean you are" said a large man with a hacking cough. It was the first time MacBean had thought not about violence being his biggest threat but rather disease.

"Hey, I don't want any trouble. Just trying to keep myself cool under this bridge."

"We own this bridge" said the large man.

"Cut the crap, OK? Bridge is free for anybody, mister" said the man with the crutches.

"You vouching for him, Buddy?"

"Yeah, I'm vouching for him. You got a problem with that?"

The large man turned and walked a few feet away into the sun but came back soon after to cool off. "Don't pay attention to that guy, big blowhard. But don't cross him if you don't need to. And don't get too close to that cough. He's not a smoker, so it could be pneumonia instead of cancer."

"Thanks, for everything. "

"Round here, don't need no thanks."

"You guys hungry?"

"No, we're on the latest diet, it's called skipping meals" said a rather heavy man who MacBean figured must be as new to this as himself, most everyone else being pretty thin.

"I got a credit at the pizza shop. I'll go get us some, if you guys want."

"Depends on whether it's just food. I mean, food to eat, or do we gotta do something in exchange for the food? We don't much like it when somebody wants something in return, like blood, or going to church" said Buddy.

"Nothing in return. I'm just hungry. And my mum taught me never to eat in front of other people without offering them some. Besides, it's a credit, you know? I got to spend it or lose it. But I do need somebody to help me carry it all back." Buddy started to get himself up.

"I'm your man" Buddy said.

"I appreciate that, but I'm not sure…"

"You ain't seen my wheels man." Buddy on his crutches walked out and to the right, and disappeared. Two minutes later he came back in a beat-up, electric wheel chair with a small wagon on the back.

MacBean laughed and said, "Let's go."

Just after getting out of ear shot of the others, MacBean turned to Buddy and asked, "Where's the closest pizza shop?"

After laughing, he answered, "Don't know who taught you to play your pizza thing that way, but they taught you well, man. Now follow me."

Later as they all sat in the dark eating pizza and drinking soda (and a few clearly drinking something stronger), MacBean quietly asked Buddy, "So, uh, you mind my asking how you lost your leg?"

"None of your business."

"Oh, you're right, sorry, I'm sorry, didn't mean nothing."

"Sure, you did, you want to feel all sad for me, it'll make you feel like a good person. Make you feel grateful for all you have. Well, you don't get to do that with me. I feel like shit, why should I help you feel better?"

"Cause I feel like shit, too. I don't know, maybe if two

people feel like shit together, they don't feel so shitty alone?"

"Maybe you feel like shit cause you're so damned stupid."

"Maybe you feel like shit cause you're so damned mean. Probably mean before you lost your leg." MacBean was amazed at how angry he'd become at a poor homeless man with one leg. *Hey, being one legged doesn't exempt you from downright rudeness. Wait a minute, maybe it does. Or maybe, just maybe, there's more wrong with this guy than just missing a leg.* "Sorry, man, I'll stop bothering you."

As MacBean walked away, the man said, "I feel like shit no matter what I do."

"So, what difference do I make?" MacBean turned around and asked.

"Jesus, I'm a Vietnam vet, OK? Lost it in Nam. Came home a drug addict. Been on and off drugs rest of my life."

"You on or off right now?"

"I'm on, but only the stuff I can get at the VA. Which isn't much, believe you me!"

"What'd you do before Nam?"

"I was a short order cook. Great job. Met a lot of good people. But you can't sit in a wheelchair and do much in a cramped diner kitchen."

"What about getting a prothesis, you know, a…"

"I know what a prothesis is, jackass. First one didn't fit good, a lot of pain. Second one fit good; it got stolen first night I was on the streets. VA got me a replacement, but I sold it for drugs. Can't get another one unless I pay for it, which of course, I can't. Besides, been without one so long, probably can't get it to fit now, anyway."

"Well, at least you got your chair. Surprised nobody's stolen it."

"Remember that large guy with the cough? Believe it or not, we're friends, did him a big favor once. Anybody steals the chair, and he finds out who, will get an ass kicking they won't forget."

"You think these guys would let me tell them a story?"

"What, like a bedtime story or something? Oh no, wait, you mean a Bible story?!"

"No, no, I mean a story about my life. It's part of what I'm doing out here."

"You did buy them pizza, so they'll probably listen. But you'll need to buy 'em some more down the road."

"You mean bribe them?"

"OK, if you want to put it that bluntly, yep. Hey, guys, this fellow wants to tell you a story, and he promises if you let him, he'll buy pizza again next week. OK?"

Mumbles of "Yeah," and "Why not" came from the group. They stayed in three or four smaller groups, but their heads turned toward MacBean as he began.

"Last bunch of guys I was with, I told about how I got my name, MacBean. I thought I'd tell you guys about my mum and dad. They came over from Scotland shortly after World War One. They were starving, I mean that literally, in Scotland, everybody was pretty much. To them, America was the land of hope and dreams. They arrived in 1924. Dad worked on the docks and Mum had a sewing business from home. She made all our clothes. Let me tell you, my dad and I were two of the best dressed men in New York City! And all their dreams *did* come true. America was the land of opportunity for them." MacBean stopped his story, realizing he was talking about how much opportunity America had to a bunch of men who were homeless for a variety of reasons. *What a dumb story to be telling.* OK, OK, I'm gonna switch gears right here in the middle of my story."

"Thank God. I know you bought the pizza and all, but this is more like one of them church stories than anything else." That was spoken by a man with dark skin and black eyes. As MacBean stared at him, anger rose up in his throat.

"You're Muslim, aren't you?" said MacBean.

"My father was Muslim; my mother was born Iranian Jew

who converted." But I don't practice it anymore. I don't know if that means I'm a Muslim or not. What do you think?"

"I hate Muslims. No, I mean, I did hate Muslims."

"For 9/11, right?"

MacBean shook his head, "Yes".

"You're not the only one. But disliking all Muslims for that would be like hating all Germans for World War Two."

"Back in the war, many did just that."

"But not now. Why?"

"Because they learned it wasn't the fault of all Germans. Not sure I agree."

"So, you hate all Germans?"

"No, I mean I think all Germans deserve some blame for the war. But I can forgive them, without forgetting. Wise man told me that once."

"So, all Muslims deserve some blame for 9/11?"

"Maybe a little bit, the ones in AL Qaeda sure do. But I'm trying very hard to forgive them. Don't you blame all Jews for the Palestinian problem?"

"AHHHH, you are much smarter than I thought! But no, I do not. Because I, personally, don't care in the least about anybody or anything in the Middle East – period."

"And you are much saner than I figured you to be."

The dark man held out his hand, which MacBean shook. "I am Joe."

"Joe? You're kidding me."

"It's really Mohammed, but since I don't practice that religion anymore, I call myself Joe."

"If not practicing the religion we're born into required another name, there would be a lot of people renaming themselves, including me."

"But I'm sure you can see that my prior religion is not just something for one day a week, it's an entire way of life for seven days a week.

"You're right, I shouldn't make light of your decision. I

seem to be saying sorry a lot today."

"Why don't you go on with another story?"

"OK, I'll tell you about how I knew I was a born businessman. When I was only around twelve or thirteen, I knew a kid who could steal a few boxes of condoms from his dad who was a distributor, and then we'd resell them individually to high school students at a tidy profit. Remember, this is back in the fifties when some guys were still shy about buying rubbers at the local drug store where the people working there knew their parents. I also found a way to steal a little bit of wine from a large wine vat and sell it in small milk cartons, again, at a tidy profit.

"And what did you do with those tidy profits?" asked Joe.

"Most of it I put in a savings account until I had enough to invest in the stock market under my dad's name. I knew even then I wanted to work on Wall Street, as a broker. Even as a kid, I knew the direction I was headed."

"So, you did it just to make the money in order to make more money?"

"Well, yeah, that's the point of most business."

"True enough. But did you have fun doing these things?"

"I did. It was fun knowing I could figure out ways to make money at a time when there weren't many ways a young kid could make much. That was fun, the figuring out part."

"So, it was really the figuring out part that made you happy. And money was a lovely byproduct."

MacBean sat very still as he pondered that statement. *Was it the figuring out part that he liked, even more than the money part? Could that be true? Why does it matter?* And yet MacBean somehow knew that it did.

A tall thin man walked into the group and sat down with a large sigh after picking up the last pizza slice in the last pizza box. "Don't know how this got here, but thank you, Lord." Throughout the group there were shouts of , "Hey" and "You're back, man" and "My man, Abraham" over emphasizing the rhyme.

"I, uh, I brought the pizza" said MacBean, unsure of whether to say it. "Thought the guys might like it, you know, and I wanted to maybe tell a story or two, about myself I mean."

"Oh, well then, thank you, Lord, for bringing us this guy who brought pizza with him."

"You're welcome."

"I wasn't talking to you." With that, the last light from surrounding electric lights were turned off, and the groups broke up, some heading off, others laying down, and others using each other as makeshift pillows. MacBean decided to take a walk before finding someplace to sleep.

About ten minutes later, as he strolled back to the group's location, something hard hit him in the back of his head and knocked him to his knees. Then he was hit in his ribs causing him to crumple over in a heap. The last thing he remembered before waking up at dawn was hearing Buddy shouting at him, "Get 'em, get 'em, kill the gooks!"

When he opened his eyes, he found Joe and Abraham staring back at him. MacBean tried to sit up but felt woozy. "Stay down a little longer. Buddy's crutch hit you pretty hard in the head. Ribs, too."

Abraham pressed on MacBean's ribs slightly. "Ohhhh, stop that" shouted MacBean.

"Probably broken, you better get to the clinic. You need to make sure you don't have a concussion or a rib that could cause a lung puncture. Come on, let's try getting up again but with me and Joe holding you up." The two men on each side of him helped MacBean to stand. "OK, I'm gonna call somebody I know who'll pick you up and take you to the clinic."

Abraham disappeared for a minute into a nearby store and came back to tell MacBean that his friend'll be here in a few minutes. "How do you know so much about this?"

"Used to be a doctor. Before the drugs and the stress got

me. About three years ago."

"There wasn't anybody could help you with that?"

"What the hell do you think an addiction is? It means you don't want help; you want the thing you're addicted to. You are so not one of us. What are you even doing here?"

"I'm trying to find myself. Yeah, I know, sounds stupid, but I know you know what I mean. Just trying to…"

"Not be an asshole. I do get that. Good luck with that."

"Thanks. No, wait, you didn't mean that did you?"

"Maybe you won't find yourself as you say. But you sure as hell will discover that whoever you are, however you lived before visiting us, that was not the "real world".

"It was as real as any other world. What I'm learning is it isn't the *only* real world."

"There may be hope for you, yet" said Joe. A yellow cab pulled up a few yards and honked. "That's your ride. Good luck, I mean that." They helped MacBean into the cab, and Joe said, "You might be better off trying someplace else than Joplin. Don't know why, but Buddy's PTSD seems to be acting up, and, in the past, when he starts hurting somebody, he usually keeps doing it, to the same guy I mean. Come back, and visit us some other time; we'll arrange a nice barbecue or something for you." Both Joe and Abraham laughed at Joe's joke. They shut the car door on MacBean, and Abraham knocked on the window for him to roll it down. MacBean did that, and Abraham pulled out of his pocket, a smashed roll of toilet paper.

"Here, man, you should take this" Abraham said as he handed it to MacBean.

"Toilet paper?"

"Seems to me, that before you can 'find yourself', you're gonna need a lot of this. Cause right now, your air of superiority, thinking you got all the answers, makes you so full of shit, man." MacBean accepted the roll and put it in his backpack.

The driver then drove off as MacBean shouted out the window, "I know I am. But self-righteousness makes people sick!"

At the Free Clinic, MacBean was wrapped up tightly with a couple of cracked ribs but none threatening a lung. He had a big lump but no concussion as far as they could tell. He gave the clinic a hundred dollars even though he didn't need to. And then he hopped the next train he could and found himself heading northeast. He could not help thinking about why he hadn't asked Joe what caused him not to be a practicing Muslim anymore, or why nobody had told him about Buddy's PTSD, or why Abraham disliked him so. *What the hell had I done that was so awful that he'd call me full of shit?* He kept going over and over in his mind what he'd said, or what he did, until his mind finally gave up and let him sleep. He had forgotten to change into khakis and polo, and more than a few passengers passed on sitting next to the bum in window seat row twelve.

...brothers don't let each other wander in the dark alone. It takes two men to make one brother.
—Israel Zangwill

He got off the train in Springfield, Massachusetts. Still reeling from Abraham's remark, MacBean decided to change into his "good" clothes at the station and find someplace for a decent lunch. He sat on a counter stool of a local diner across the river in West Springfield, feeling on top of the world, as he ate his large and juicy bacon burger, the kind requiring more napkins than a summer ice cream cone. It dawned on him how much his definition of a decent lunch had changed. *OK, Abraham, maybe you are honest Abe, and maybe I am full of shit, but I'm learning. Never was a fast learner at anything but numbers.* When he finished, he changed in the small diner bathroom back into his hobo clothes. As he changed, he smiled remembering when he had to explain to Jesús just what a hobo was. He also felt old but then remembered Jesús saying so seriously, "I was taught to respect my elders, MacBean," it made him laugh, laugh so loud in fact that as he walked down the sidewalk, he was sure someone would be calling the police about a crazy old bum on Railroad Street.

First stop was the public library, a branch on the town outskirts. There he looked at a map of the city in order to get his bearings and figure out where to walk. He noticed a couple of parks and decided to walk to the one furthest away from the city center. He'd been told that police usually would leave you alone as long as you weren't seen as harassing downtown shoppers. When he arrived at the park, he sat on a bench and just watched, hoping to see some other homeless guys in order to follow them. Eventually, he saw one who was stopping at every trash can in the park, apparently. It continued to surprise MacBean how much edible food people threw away in a day, sometimes even wrapped food, as if taking it with them was too much of a burden to bear. He saw the man pick out wrapped twinkies from one trash can, and a sandwich of some kind, only half eaten from another. *Maybe it's a Reuben.* MacBean was glad for the man that the day's pickings were bountiful. There was a trash can next to MacBean's bench, and when the man reached it, MacBean said to him, "Looks like a decent day."

"You need something?"

"No, no, but thanks for offering. No, wait, I do need something, but not to eat. Where's a good place to sleep? You know any?"

"Yeah, I do. But if I tell people, then it won't be so good anymore, will it? Sorry, man."

"You're right, man, I get it. Just that, I'm new to this place, just passing through though, won't be staying long."

"You got any money or drink?"

"If I tell people, then I won't have it anymore, will I? Sorry, man."

"Just thinking we could do a deal. You give me a drink, and I show you where to sleep."

"Sounds fair to me. But you have to show me first."

The man nodded and motioned for MacBean to follow him. As the sun set, he followed the man into the woods of the park, then out the back of the woods, down a hill or two, and back into a stand of trees in somebody's yard. "Are you kidding me? I can't sleep in somebody's yard!"

"Safest place to sleep. Sleep after they've all gone to bed, get up before any of them do. Look up there, up in the tree." MacBean looked up and saw a treehouse. *Damn, an actual treehouse. This is cool. But is it safe?*

"We can't go there yet, it's too early. I'll meet you here tonight, be sure you got that drink for me. And don't follow me, I got to do some business.:

As the man walked away, MacBean watched him disappear. And he walked the other way, but trying to make note of how to get back here. He didn't even care that it was risky to sleep in somebody's yard. The idea of spending a night in a treehouse made him feel like a little kid, and he liked that feeling. Late that night, MacBean managed to find his way back to the yard, made sure there were no lights on in the house, climbed the wooden slats nailed onto the tree, and entered into the covered treehouse. The man was already there, snoring so loudly MacBean wondered whether he would be able to sleep at all. But soon after laying his head on his backpack, wrapped a strap tightly around his wrist so as to wake up if anybody was trying to steal it, he fell fast asleep.

At dawn, the man shook MacBean awake. "You got that drink you promised me?"

MacBean rummaged in his backpack and took out a couple of nips and handed them to the guy. He had figured out that cigarettes and nips were an excellent currency in the homeless world. MacBean purchased his, but no one ever questioned where the items came from, assuming it part of their code never to talk about stolen goods. The man gulped the first nip down and then the second. His eyes glistened as he told MacBean, “I wasn’t always a bum, ya know. Used to be an electrician, a damned good one, too. In the union and everything.”

“I could tell you were an educated man.” MacBean had learned not to ask questions directly, but to say something positive and let a man decide whether or not to talk further.

“My wife got sick, real sick. Cancer.”

“Sorry, man, that’s gotta be really tough.”

“I couldn’t pay the bills. They gave me a schedule, ya know, so I could pay every month. But by then I had started drinking. I knew I shouldn’t, but it was just all so much to take. Then I lost my job. I’m just glad she died before she found that out.”

“And now you can’t stop the drinking. I hear you, I been there myself.”

“You? You don’t look like the usual bums. Something about you’s different.”

“My wife died in 9/11. Started drinking…a lot.”

“It’s hard, man, ain’t it? So hard to go on without. . .it’s the regrets, the things that you can never make up for. Spent my life telling her, ‘I’ll make up for it, I promise’. But. of course, I never did. And then. . .too late.”

“Not too late to make up for other things.”

“Whatcha mean?”

“I’m traveling around, trying to tell my story to whoever’ll listen. That’s kind of how I’m trying to make up for it.”

“I knew you weren’t just anybody. What’s your name anyway?”

“JoJo MacBean.”

“I’m Archie.”

“Ever heard of me?”

“No, sorry.”

“No problem. I appreciate you telling me your story,

Archie."

"I lied, man, I lied." The booze was clearly taking effect. "My wife died, but I started the drinking way before that. And drugs, too, when I got shot in Vietnam, and when I came home. I ain't never been the same since."

"Why'd you lie?"

"I got me a Purple Heart for Christ's sake. I'm ashamed, man, ashamed of what I've become. I've dishonored the Marines. Don't like people to know that."

"No way, man. You haven't dishonored anybody. If anybody's dishonored anybody, it's me that's dishonored you. I'm one of those guys that found a way to get out of the draft." MacBean lowered his head realizing he'd said his secret before thinking whether he should.

"A draft dodger?"

"Not exactly. But close. No, no, I mean yes, I was. You see, I've spent a life making excuses for myself. I had motion sickness once or twice as a kid, but I grew out of it. My boss found a doctor that would sign off on it being a serious, ongoing thing. You see, I was an important man at the firm."

"You mean making money was important."

"It was. It is," MacBean hesitated, "isn't it?"

"Well, you weren't alone, in draft dodging I mean."

"At the time, I thought I was right."

"At the time. Three words that have been said by every person alive."

"And always with regret."

"Maybe you *are* a guy with a story to tell. I know where a bunch of guys meet after dark. We'll go there tonight. But don't say anything about this treehouse or I swear, I'll go all Marine on you, MacBean." MacBean gasped and then exhaled when Archie laughed.

"Do you and the guys like pizza?"

It was a hot July afternoon, and the sun shone brightly on the Connecticut River as Archie and MacBean carried several pizza boxes and soda six packs to a place underneath the Memorial Bridge in West Springfield, Massachusetts. He'd landed in West Springfield originally because someone on the train in New York had said he should see the Basketball Hall of Fame in Springfield. Meeting Archie in the park was about the best luck MacBean could remember, outside of Sam Slade being his friends' father. MacBean had decided to stay a while because of Archie and because of this under-bridge area. It seemed to him that the group of homeless folks gathered there were as close as he would ever find to a hobo lifestyle. He spent the whole of the summer in West Springfield, having found a relatively receptive audience for his storytelling. Of course, regular pizza buying didn't hurt anything except his wallet, a fact that was beginning to concern him a bit. But as time passed, MacBean discovered Sorrento's, a restaurant whose owner welcomed stock tips as much as the deli owners did. Not only could MacBean exchange his tips for pizzas, but the owner hooked MacBean up with the owner of Roma's, another restaurant in a nearby town that did wedding catering. MacBean and Archie, along with a couple others MacBean invited each time, would go in early on the morning after a wedding to eat some of the leftovers like rib marsala and scrod marinara. It wasn't that easy to get there from West Springfield, but it was worth it every time. And it became kind of a game among the homeless guys as to who MacBean would invite along to the "hobo wedding." It wasn't any mystery, MacBean simply invited the guys least receptive to his storytelling and the least likely to tell their own stories, until eventually even the most reluctant among the group would ask for a story or tell one in order to increase his invitation potential.

In some quarters, he'd become a topic of conversation. He was especially clean for a bum, exceptionally smart, and always considerate. He didn't eat out of garbage containers, well, not often anyway. As usual, hungry men could depend on people who threw away perfectly good wrapped food that had never been opened. MacBean was not the least bit revolted by eating those tasty items. He didn't sleep much like many homeless guys he knew. He was the only one that didn't have the stench of "Bondi's Island" lingering on his clothes. He bought some clothes at Salvation Army and Savers, golf shirts and sweats mostly, but sometimes nice khakis and Docker shoes to replace the ones he'd been forced to wear too often to maintain a "normal person" look. He looked for name brands, LL Bean, Land's End, Lacoste, not because he cared about the name but because it meant he was spending his money wisely. JoJo MacBean had become the preppiest bum you'd ever want to see.

When Archie and MacBean put down their pizzas and sodas, MacBean said "This is the life, hey, Archie? Pure freedom."

"Are you kidding? I'm sick of eating out of trash cans, smelling bad all the time, collecting cans and bottles for spare change and carrying my belongings around. If I gotta wash my clothes, I have to use the river. It's not the life I planned." Some of the other guys agreed with Archie. They didn't seem too pleased with their lives either.

MacBean snapped back. "Look, it doesn't have to be that way. Believe it or not you have control of your own life. We all do."

"How so?" Archie asked. "You don't think we'd like to be sitting in an air-conditioned office right now? Then go home and snuggle up with the one you love after a day of work. How about going to the movie tonight honey? And having the money to do these things."

"Archie, it isn't all that rosy on the other side of the fence. I've been there".

"Spoken like only a rich man could." Archie and the other men were usually amused at MacBean's comments, but a few were now clearly angry. After all, Archie and the others had been homeless for a while, some for most of their adulthood.

Alcohol, drugs, poverty, mental illness, or even just medical bills, these were real battles they had fought and thus far lost.

"What the hell!" said Jake. "We got all kinds of time to kill. Why don't you tell us another story about your life before you became. . . one of us", he said while chuckling. "Maybe you'll reform us. We all know that's what you're trying to do, MacBean."

"No, Jake, that's not it at all. I'm trying to tell my story so I understand it myself."

"Then stop preaching, just tell it."

"I don't mean it to be preaching, it just comes out that way sometimes."

"Maybe that's part of what you need to understand about yourself," Archie said.

MacBean replied, "I can always depend on you, Archie, to keep me on track. But listen, guys, we've got time on our side. That is one thing you don't get enough of when you live the kind of life I did. Everything, go, go, go, rush, rush, rush. No one has time for anything anymore. So, what story should I tell tonight? You've heard most of my life by now. Hard to remember what's left to tell."

"Hah, we know you well enough by now, MacBean, if it's about you, you've forgotten nothing!" MacBean smiled but felt uncomfortable knowing that was probably true. The sun was now high overhead and MacBean laid his head back against the cool cement bridgework and said "To be continued later, my friends. This man needs a nap before his pizza. But you better leave me a slice, OK?! Not like last time. Or else next time, I'll buy that pineapple one you all hate!"

An hour later, as MacBean woke up and stretched, Archie said, "So tell us, MacBean, you told us you been married four times, but not much else about women."

"Yeah, if you were so rich, you must have had lots of women! Even if you are ugly!" said one of the guys.

"Ahhh, let me start at the beginning. Back in junior high and high school, I liked girls but I had not the foggiest idea how to handle them or approach them. HAH, still don't. I wasn't part of the "in" crowd, even though I ended up being one of the top students in my high school class. Still, I was anything but popular. Been married four times though. I must have had something!"

"Yeah, a few million!" Archie shouted, to which everyone, including MacBean, laughed.

"True enough. Except my first love came before those millions, and my last love came in spite of them." MacBean grew quiet and a sadness crept across his face that silenced even Archie.

"Did you really go to Harvard? And you're out here now like one of us?"

"I did not realize at that time that maybe I rose up the ladder too fast and that I wasn't handling the situation properly because I was still quite immature personally. Of course, there's no telling that to a twenty-two-year-old. There's no telling them anything at all! They already think they know everything. And that included me."

"Still does sometimes" said Jake.

"Get back to the girls! Give us a tale of love," MacGregor yelled.

His name was Greg, but MacBean had dubbed him MacGregor on his first visit because MacBean had initially mistaken his odd eating habits as a result of a thriftiness worthy of any Scotchman. He had seen MacGregor eat a banana peel because he had said he didn't want to waste food. Later that night MacGregor told him that he wasn't being thrifty, he just couldn't stop bad habits. He'd been abused as a child and made to eat garbage, like banana peels, and at times could not resist a compulsion to do so again. Of course, some homeless had to eat garbage, there wasn't anything else to eat. But MacGregor never ate like that unless his compulsion kicked in. Later, MacBean dubbed him "Sir" MacGregor because he didn't know what else he could do for a man so broken in spirit as to eat garbage when he didn't need to.

"Tales of woe, my friends, and tales of love. I had become a success on Wall Street, but I had no personal life. With my money and my growing Wall Street notoriety, I was becoming that well known creature called a chick-magnet. Of course, those particular chicks were not the kind of women to bring home to mum and dad. What parents wouldn't want this laddie-boy for a son-in-law? I was a star on the rise. Looking back, this was the time my ego was starting to get out of control."

"Only then?!" someone shouted with laughter.

"A big ego's nothing to laugh at. I went through three marriages with women who had no sense of who they were, either. And it led us to some dark places. Although my third wife, Angela, has enough of my money to keep her dark places quite illuminated for the rest of her life. She could buy her own power plant if she wanted to!"

"What, a smart guy like you never heard of a pre-nup?"

"You can be too smart for your good sometimes; you think you know better than everybody else."

"So, the smart guy's actually stupid, you're saying" shouted someone.

"He is if he doesn't listen. I never listened. And so, I never learned. But you know guys, I really got the good life now. I'm in my fifties, but I feel twenty years younger. I have no bills to pay, no everyday real pressure, I get a nice meal now and then, and I have traveled throughout most of the United States. I've made some friends along the way, and I met all kinds of interesting people. What more could I ask for?" MacBean asked with a grin that had once graced Time magazine. "I'm doing it again, sorry. I really don't mean it's easy for you guys, I know it's not. But I do feel happier right now sitting here than I've felt since my wife, Maria, died. I apologize if I sound naïve. I'm not. It's just the truth. And I feel more relaxed than I've felt my whole life. Guess you're right, just plain stupid?"

"YES!" shouted fifteen homeless men in both jest and earnest.

"But who's Maria? We've never heard you mention any Maria before," said MacGregor.

"And you won't again. Some things are sacred."

Late that autumn night, Archie and MacBean sat in their treehouse talking quietly about their plan to travel around the county together. Archie had stopped drinking and was trying mightily to keep sober, and MacBean saw it was helping the man to talk about the other places they could go. They would winter in the warmer states and come back "home" to West Springfield in the spring. One of the conversations that night was about Joplin. It turned out that Archie had also been to Joplin with another Marine buddy. MacBean had then told Archie that he'd met a man named Buddy, who was a disabled vet with PTSD.

"Holy crap, my friend, he was named Buddy, and he was disabled. He didn't have PTSD, least not when I knew him. Do you think it could be the same guy?"

"Was yours a short order cook?"

"Hot damn, MacBean. That's him, that's my Buddy. Oh, man, I'd love to go see him again. Let's put Joplin on our list, maybe on our way back. I'd love to get Buddy to come with us."

"I just have to find some computer work, so I can buy you a train pass, too. I got a lead yesterday from overhearing somebody in the park. It's a small mom and pop store that can't figure out their new system, and they kept complaining that the kid from the company treats them like they're idiots. I'm going there tomorrow to see if they'd like to give me a chance to help them with it."

Sure enough, the mom and pop were only too happy to find someone who didn't treat them like techno Neanderthals, even if they were ones. MacBean also asked if they had any other leads for him, and they referred him to a pawn shop that often-received PCs and Macs but had nobody on staff that knew enough about how to fix them and sell them. MacBean became the pawn shop's tech guy on the weekends. At the end of four months, he had made enough to buy the Amtrak pass for Archie and pocket a little more to help with pizzas at other future stops.

Travel not to find yourself, but to remember who you've been all along. — Anonymous

In November, 2005, the two men hopped on a train at night and got a good night's sleep, arriving at a small city the next morning. For the next six months, MacBean and Archie traveled around the country, stopping where they wanted. A few of the places, mostly the larger cities, did not have friendly homeless people, due to the competition for limited resources and a more harried police force. But most places were of the "live and let live" variety that meant some homeless wanted nothing to do with them, and other homeless were as welcoming and friendly as imaginable.

Maybe there aren't any more hobos in America, but I was right that being a hobo is as much a way of thinking as it is a literal lifestyle. The closed boxcars had made that life impossible, but for someone like MacBean, who grew up listening to his dad tell him stories that he'd heard from his friends, the hobo life meant freedom extraordinaire. If you felt above all – free - in being homeless, as opposed to desperate, then you qualified for hobo-ship. In most parts of the country, although MacBean managed to make friends almost everywhere, there was the understandable, but decided, whiff of desperation in most homeless gatherings. In fact, in most places, there were no gatherings at all, except by grifter gangs who had turned begging into a 21st century art form. And of course, MacBean wasn't jumping on and off boxcars, he had purchased that Amtrak pass. But he no longer thought of any place as home other than West Springfield. He and Archie slept many a night in a culvert or a park. MacBean was glad Archie was with him, the old man was much smarter in reading people than MacBean ever was.

But part of living a life of pure freedom was not paying close attention to where your train was headed. And although he made every effort to eat only what he found or was given, desperation occasionally called for a meal at IHop or the Colonel's. MacBean never failed to also bring pizzas to his homeless friends whenever he'd succumbed to the call of fried chicken or all you can eat pancakes. In fact, his homeless friends began to very much root for a downfall, not understanding that MacBean was disappointed in himself, even as they were just plain hungry.

And everywhere he could, MacBean would tell a story about his life, most often about how much money he wasted, how little he understood about people, and being selfish, even if he hadn't known it *at the time.* He also heard their stories. All so different, all so much the same. Something happened, and life was never the same again. What surprised him was that so often that "something" occurred before the addictions, not vice versa. So often, the addiction was an understandable response to pain, physical or mental. Understandable, but not effective. In Charleston, MacBean told the story about the two guys whom he'd laid off at KBL.

Under a bridge in Charleston, the humidity was stifling. MacBean and Archie liked it here, the people were friendly, almost gentile. And oddly enough, the homeless folks had some of that same politeness. It was odd to see a guy on a street corner say, "Thank you so much, ma'am", or "God bless you, ma'am; the Lord be with you," or "I know you got troubles, too" when someone would walk by without dropping anything into their cup.

"You mean you didn't care about those two guys losing their jobs?" asked Bubba.

"I knew them both, from rich families, I wasn't worried for them".

"Still, you worked twelve, fourteen-hour days, and if they had families, they probably couldn't do that"

"Couldn't or wouldn't. There's a difference, Bubba. Anybody going into that business knows what's expected of them."

"But did they have families? Did you even know?"

MacBean hadn't known, nor had he cared at the time. But Bubba was right, of course. Over and over and over, he would tell a story with a lesson that would turn out not to be the lesson he'd planned. And over and over and over, he would be grateful for that.

In April, the pair ended up back in Joplin. They headed straight from the train station to the place MacBean remembered. He wondered if Joe, Abraham, Jesús, or Buddy were still around. Archie told him not to look too happy to see them again, it might make them targets of guys prone to jealousy. But when he saw Abraham, MacBean felt an overwhelming feeling of gratitude to the man for his prior honesty. He only hoped he'd had enough time to lessen his load so to speak. Abraham was astonished to see MacBean and gave him a warm hug. His words were not as warm. "How in the hell are you still alive?!"

"Hard to kill somebody so ornery. That's why you're so old."

Abraham laughed and said, "I'd rather be ornery than full of shit."

"You remembered!" Now MacBean was laughing, too. "Abraham, meet my traveling companion, Archie. He's come to visit Buddy."

"Oh, I'm sorry, man, but Buddy died. Last January. Froze to death. We had record lows, and we all tried to get him to come to the shelter with us, but you know him, he was in and out of Nam in his head, he stopped listening altogether to anybody but the scared grunt he was back in Nam. You in Nam with him, Archie?"

"Yeah. And later, when we both landed in Joplin and worked at Dinah's Café, him as a cook and me as a dishwasher."

"Archie got a Purple Heart for saving Buddy and another kid."

"Oh, hell, you're Baldy! Buddy told me all about Baldy!"

"Baldy?! "said a surprised MacBean.

"Short for Archibald, OK? You ever call me that again and I'll pop you one."

"What did Buddy say about Bal, I mean, Archie?"

"Best friend he ever had. But you had to go back East to see, who was it?"

"My daughter."

"You never told me you had a daughter," said MacBean.

"And you haven't told me much about Maria either."

"Joe still around?" MacBean asked.

"Not Joe anymore. He's back to Mohammed now."

"Really? How'd that happen?"

"You can ask him yourself. He works at the food kitchen at his mosque. I think you might of had something to do with it."

"Not likely. But I would like to see him."

Archie had wandered just a short way off from the conversation, and MacBean knew enough to let him be. Archie had spent a lot of time in the past six months of traveling around, telling MacBean how much he enjoyed Buddy's company, that he'd once been one of the funniest and nicest men on earth. How Buddy had always said grace before eating and yet knew swear words Archie had never even heard of before. MacBean and Abraham sat down with a couple other guys when Archie wandered back and sat next to MacBean. "I didn't mean it. About never calling me Baldy again. In fact,

I think, I'd like it if everybody would call me that now. Every time somebody calls me that, I'll remember Buddy and all the good times. There were some, and that's what I want to hold onto, what I have to hold onto." And from then on, he was Baldy.

The next morning, Baldy, MacBean, and Abraham visited the food kitchen for breakfast. There was Mohammed serving up the eggs. He now had well kempt beard and clean clothes, and when they approached him, he asked someone to take over for him, and he motioned the group to take a seat at one of the round tables.

"It is amazing to see you again. I never thought I would," said Mohammed.

"Or me you, Joe, I mean Mohammed, excuse me. This seems like a trip for changing names, doesn't it?"

Mohammed looked a bit confused but went on, "It is because of you, MacBean, oh, you haven't changed your name, have you?"

"No, no, no, still MacBean. But I hope, really hope, that I've changed even if my name hasn't."

"So, you have been continuing your hajj?"

"My what?"

"Your hajj. Your pilgrimage. To find yourself."

"Oh, yes, my hajj. Baldy and I have been all over this country since leaving Joplin. He's kept me out of trouble."

"And he has kept me in pizza," Baldy said laughing.

"And you returned to see me and Abraham and Jesús?"

"Baldy wanted to see Buddy again. They were in the same unit in Vietnam. We were so sorry to be too late."

"It is never too late to visit dear friends. They may appear to be gone, but their spirits live on in our memories."

"May I ask, when did you find Islam again?"

"When you left, and Abraham gave you that toilet paper, it made me laugh. But then he looked at me and said, 'Why are you laughing, Joe? If you ever leave, you'll need an entire truck load of TP.' I was taking myself so seriously, I'd forgotten that I was no better than you at understanding myself. I was so sanctimonious. I was living a life away from what gave my life its meaning and then thinking I was doing something admirable instead of just fool-hardy. It is hard, nearly impossible, for any of us to find our way in this world without some help from the next one. But I am preaching now, sorry, I still can't help myself sometimes, forgive me!"

"You're forgiven, my friend. And for everything."

"You've gotten over it, MacBean, the hatred?"

"Had to. The hobos I met along the way kept calling me out on my bullcrap, every step of the way, including my thinking anybody but twisted individuals were responsible for Maria's death."

"We two are the luckiest men on earth, to be given our lives back."

"And still with time to live it," MacBean added.

"A gift from men with far greater problems than our own."

"Who else would we have listened to?"

"You have learned, MacBean. How long are you staying?"

"Not long I'm afraid. I've been traveling over a year, I'm ready to head home."

"New York?"

"No, my home now is West Springfield, in Massachusetts."

"You and Baldy will come home with me tonight to have a meal, and to sleep. I won't take no for an answer."

"You won't have to!" said Archie.

It was a wonderful evening. The beds were comfortable, and with the window open, a cool breeze came through. MacBean slept peacefully and woke up to a soft, rainy dawn, and the whisper of prayers in the next room. Both MacBean and Baldy helped make food and then served it in the food kitchen that morning as a thank you to Mohammed, yet they both felt the same homesickness and knew they would be on their way early the next day.

That evening, Baldy was trying to remember all the places they had been in the last several months so he could keep a list eventually. "Did we stop in Poughkeepsie?"

"No, it was Schenectady." That went on for a while with other names before MacBean declared lights out. Early the next morning, he said his goodbyes for a second time to Abraham and Mohammed, each couple realizing they would probably never see the other two men again. On the train, Baldy started his town name game again, and MacBean tried to keep his patience from wearing out.

They weren't planning on making any stops along the way except to change a train. But when they pulled into Buffalo someone had said that the greatest Jewish deli in all the world, bar none, even New York, was in this city. And it was called Bloomberg's. There was no way MacBean was passing on that. Baldy and MacBean looked at each other and knew they'd be getting off for at least an afternoon of stuffing themselves.

And stuff themselves they did. Blintzes, Reubens, pastrami, egg creams, even celery soda. *Good thing we're headed to West Springfield where I can make some money fixing computers, because I just spent an outrageous amount on a Jewish feast.*

LOST AND FOUND

Late that night, the two decided to take a walk to work off some of the calories they'd had earlier that day. They were going to board a night train to Albany and catch a train to Springfield from there. They were so excited about reaching "home", they lost track of where they were walking, and found themselves a bit lost. A homeless person is never fully lost because where they came from isn't any more important than where they're headed. They decided to walk behind a strip mall where two strangers jumped out from a dumpster and knocked them both out. When Baldy came to, he immediately checked for their backpacks, both of them gone. Then he saw MacBean lying there and shouted, "Don't die on me, MacBean, please don't die!"

"I'm not dying, I'm crying. They got my backpack, didn't they? All we had, my ID, what little cash I had, my train pass, all of it was in my backpack, Baldy."

"Don't worry, I'll handle it. I've been without all of that stuff before, remember? I've been a real homeless person. I'll figure this out. Let me take the lead for a change."

"But I need ID and walking around cash. I need to get back to New York, to find somebody who can help me get a new ID and some cash for clothes and food, just enough to get back to West Springfield."

"OK, New York City it is. You know who to see?"

"Yeah, I got a hunch there's one person at Columbia that might help us."

So, take the lead Baldy did. He found a truck stop and a trucker willing to let them ride in his empty truck as far as Albany. From there, Baldy begged some people for money to buy a bus ticket. Probably the first time anyone heard that when it was actually true. And a single person came through with half the fare. They slept in the basement stairs of a library for the night. Next morning, Baldy started begging again and made some more. Several more nights were spent sleeping in various places in the city. Baldy also managed to locate a church that had clothes to give away, and they found some clean jeans and tees in the bunch. They finally boarded the bus for New York City after living eighteen days of the genuine homeless life, a time MacBean spent being so scared knowing this was "real" that he wondered how in the world anybody ever survived it. He said that to Baldy, who told him, "Many of them don't survive. I don't mean they die physically; I mean they die emotionally. Survival actually requires it."

When they finally reached the office of Professor Rivers Fitzpatrick, luck was with them; office hours were in session. Rivers looked up from her desk, stood up, tossed off her glasses, ran to MacBean and threw her arms around him. "Oh Jesus,

I've been so worried about you." Then she gave him a slight shove. "I said find yourself, not lose yourself. Where the hell have you been?!"

"This is Baldy. Baldy, this is Rivers. And I've been everywhere." MacBean gave her a condensed version of his travels, and ended by telling her about losing his little cash, rail pass, and any ID, including an emergency credit card. Rivers found out how to let the credit card company know to cancel the card. She found on the web the procedure for a new ID card, and she went to the ATM to withdraw cash to give him before he left.

That night they slept at her apartment on her sofa and floor. They told her they were headed first to Providence and then back to West Springfield. MacBean was planning on finding work there doing something or other with computers while Baldy would find a job as a short order cook. The two men were planning on becoming roommates and possibly taking on a third roommate if they could find someone they trusted. Baldy had told MacBean that he'd wanted to stop off in Providence because he'd heard from some other vets that his old CO was at the VA Hospital there. But actually, Baldy wanted to stop there because he wanted to see if there was any way to get into that hospital. He hadn't told MacBean just how poorly he was feeling.

The next day MacBean went about replacing his ID and his emergency ATM card. He couldn't wait to buy some pizzas for the guys under the bridge, even if he wasn't going to be one of them anymore. Of course, the economy wasn't doing all that well; he and Baldy could be one of them at any time.

The following morning, Rivers said, "MacBean, before you head back, I need to tell you something, something sad."

"What? Jeez, you look really sad. What is it?"

"Your friend, Sam Slade, is in hospice care, end stage of Parkinson's. I was at Bloomberg's last week and heard some of the brokers talking about him."

MacBean felt a curtain of sadness drawn down over him. "Hospice, that means. . ."

"Is there some way I can reach you to let you know when he dies? You might want to try and make it to his service."

"I doubt I could do that."

"Why can't you? "

"I'm too ashamed. And I don't have good clothes to wear, I'd be embarrassed. It's not my world anymore."

"You have nothing to be embarrassed about. And I can help you find a suit."

"No, no, I don't think so, Rivers, really. Besides, I just have my little flip phone with me and coverage isn't too good, and..."

"And here I was thinking you had learned something on your travels. But you're willing to let a man who had as much influence in your life as anyone short of your parents, die without paying your respects. In fact, what you should do is march over to that hospice right now and say thank you to that man before you leave, before *he* leaves! Then it won't be such a big deal not to go to his service."

"I, I couldn't, I just..."

"Do you want to feel about Sam Slade the same way you do about Sol Bloomberg?" Rivers looked around on her desk for a piece of paper and handed it to MacBean. "It's the address. Swear to God, if you don't go, you will never forgive yourself. And I will never forgive you. Now go, just go!"

MacBean put the paper in his pocket, walked behind the desk and kissed Rivers tenderly. She opened a desk drawer and rummaged in it and handed him three hundred-dollar bills.

"It was a good kiss, but you really don't need to pay me" MacBean chuckled.

Rivers gave him a playful hit on his shoulder. "Wise guy, it's for a taxi to the hospice, and whatever else you might need right away. You'll pay me back some day, I'll make sure of that."

"Thanks. I'll see you, well, sooner or later." He and Baldy

walked out of the building and Rivers felt tears coming down her cheeks. She didn't know whether she was happy he was going to visit Sam Slade or sad he was leaving her, or perhaps a bit of both.

MacBean walked in to see a man barely recognizable as Sam, physically. Yet, he found a man changed hardly at all in spirit. *How can he be so happy when he's dying?* The two men talked for about two hours about their mutual histories, about Wall Street, about Jack, about how their pasts had made them who they were, and what a man needs to feel like a man. MacBean related his hobo journey to Sam, who laughed at the toilet paper episodes. He also thanked Sam for doing all that he did for MacBean. Sam was becoming clearly exhausted by the visit, and the nurse wanted MacBean to leave after an hour, but Sam had said to her, "What am I staying alive for if not to say goodbye to my dearest friends?" Sam could see confusion on MacBean's face and he asked, "You're wondering why I'm in such good spirits aren't you? Well, it's a fact the morphine helps!" And they both laughed as heartily as they could. Then Sam continued, "It's not morphine, it's being at peace with my decisions. I made some mistakes, some big ones, and I've asked for forgiveness for them. I've also made some good decisions, some very good ones and I'm grateful for that. I've also got a legacy, MacBean. My foundation will outlast me, outlast you, and probably outlast your grandchildren, who knows, maybe outlast your great great grandchildren. And it will do some good for people. Lord above, what right has any man to ask for more?" As Sam then closed his eyes to sleep, he said, "I'm sorry, but I can't keep my eyes open. Forgive me."

"That's OK, Sam, you get some sleep now." MacBean was grateful he was able to tell Sam about buying pizza for hungry men, but also grateful he didn't have to admit to his old friend that he hadn't yet done a daily good deed as promised.

"Safe journey to you, my son."

MacBean softly said, "I love you, Sam, safe journey to you

as well." MacBean tiptoed out of his room to find Baldy sitting in a small waiting area. When MacBean saw him, he broke down in tears, and Baldy held him while he wept.

Late that day, Baldy and MacBean were on a train headed to Providence. MacBean had gone from a completely structured life to one with little structure at all. And he liked it! It felt to him that he now had all the time in the world. He had thoughts of Maria less frequently, and when he did, they sometimes brought a smile to his face. He knew he would always feel sadness just as Sam never remembered Jack without sadness, but like Sam, he realized that sadness is what makes one grateful for the time you have. The alcoholism was well in control, there was no more depression or feeling sorry for himself. MacBean woke up each morning, sometimes even with a smile on his face, thankful for yet another day. He began to wonder what kind of life was in store for him during his remaining years on earth. And his thoughts turned to Rivers often, no longer with any guilt but with appreciation that in Baldy and Rivers he had the two most remarkable friends a person could have.

They stepped off the train in Providence, and Baldy said, "Let's head to the VA right away."

"What's your hurry? Let's get something to eat first."

"Yeah, yeah, sure. I'm just worried about my CO."

They ate at the mall across from the train station and then totally splurged on a taxi to the VA. When they walked in, Baldy told MacBean to sit in the waiting room while he tried to find out where or if his CO was here. About five minutes after Baldy had left, MacBean's head slumped over, and he fell asleep. When he woke up two hours later, it was dark outside, and MacBean felt a rising panic. As he stood up to walk over to an information desk, Baldy appeared, clearly upset and with eyes red. "Hey, buddy, what's wrong? Are you, you know, too late?" said MacBean.

"No, goddammit, I'm not too late. Not for my CO anyway.

Too late for me though."

"What's that supposed to mean?"

"I'm sorry, MacBean, but I didn't come here for my CO; I was hoping to get some meds here, but they've got a waiting list a mile long before I can see somebody."

MacBean stood frozen, trying to process the meaning of Baldy's words. His brain knew what they meant, but his heart was refusing to understand.

"You're not sick, why do you need…" as MacBean's words trailed off. "Why didn't you tell me the truth?" he whispered to Baldy.

"Cause I know how much you're planning on us going back to West Springfield and starting our lives over."

"How sick are you?"

"Not even sure myself. But I can't breathe like I used to."

"And they can't see you? What good is a VA Hospital if you can't get help when you're sick?"

"Hey, don't get me started. Let's just go."

"But what are you going to do? You need medicine and stuff, right? Let me talk to somebody."

"No, man, no. The vets ahead of me are sicker than me. And some got families, too. Let 'em go ahead of me; it's OK."

"NO. IT'S NOT OK! And you got family – ME!"

Baldy grabbed MacBean in a long bear hug. The two men walked out of the hospital and strolled the streets until they found a small covered place under the library steps where they could rest for the night. Early the next day, they boarded the train for West Springfield.

Life in West Springfield was still a combination of hobo living and working on computers. Baldy had found a part time job not as a short order cook, but dishwasher. It was easy enough for him to still handle but not enough to help much with a future apartment rental, so he and MacBean still often found themselves sleeping outdoors, or in a cheap room, or on a train. Sometimes, they would just take an overnight train somewhere to spend the day and take an overnight train back to Springfield. But they had a plan. Or at least they pretended to have a plan, as though Baldy's illness was something well into the future. Baldy didn't want to spoil MacBean's plans, and MacBean wanted Baldy to spend whatever time was left in positive ways. That plan kept them going. Any night someone would listen, MacBean would relate the stories from his life, usually stories that made it clear that he was an immature kid until well into his thirties, but he had a fine business mind and a well-meaning heart. But that heart had often taken a back seat to the fine business mind.

5

STEALING FROM DEAD PEOPLE

2005-2008

The market began 2005 at 10783 and ended 2008 at 8776

One day, MacBean was changing his shoes. *Why am I still keeping this?* He had always put the KBL client list in two parts in the bottoms of his shoes. The fact that it hadn't been in his knapsack and thus stolen kept him asking, *Is there a reason I still have it?* Many of his wealthy clients from the past were quite old now, if still living at all. *What could keeping this list possibly do for me now?* He answered himself when he finished building a small portable computer from some spare parts that he'd gathered from a couple dumps and two or three small businesses in the area. *What better way for me to spend my time than building a database to keep abreast of my past clients just in case I should ever need that.* He inputted their names, addresses, and Social Security numbers. He also inputted where they held their bank accounts plus their approximate liquid net worth at the time he was let go. Of course, KBL did not know that he had taken this information. MacBean never used the term "stolen" when thinking on this, feeling that he had built up that client list and was entitled to have it. MacBean also kept track on the web of where they lived, and even noted their approximate height and weight when he knew them as an exercise in keeping his memory sharp. MacBean was so good at obtaining this type of information that he felt it possible he knew more about these people than the government did.

He also kept up with the latest technology in the computer industry and always made sure that his computer had the latest components he could obtain. He was able to get access to the latest software for little or no cost by bargaining for it in exchange for work. Several times, he updated the client file for changes of address, divorces, spouses, and some of the latest events that his old clients were involved with.

In the fall of 2005, MacBean picked up the Wall Street Journal in the trash outside of a Starbucks. Sam's passing was on the front page of the paper, a long article about his business career that extended to another page. *What a brilliant and kind man, one who had become a real mensch.* MacBean smiled thinking of Sam and Bloomberg up in heaven, somewhere, having a Reuben with Bernstein (at least MacBean hoped Harvey was up there). He remembered how impressed he was with the brokers at Bloomberg's Deli when he was growing up, but no one could ever match Sam in sheer class. The Wall Street Journal article stated that Sam's services would be in Philadelphia, and he would be laid to rest there two days hence.

MacBean didn't feel guilty about not attending the services since he had said his goodbye to Sam, and, yet, he felt compelled to pay his respects, genuine, heart-felt respects, for a great man. The next day, he and Baldy hopped on a bus for Philly. *How could I do this? I'm not part of that world anymore. Do I want to see a lot of brokers in their Italian suits and expensive shoes, lauding it over old, broken down MacBean?* The closer they came to Philly, the more MacBean realized he wasn't as ready as he thought to face people who knew him before his hobo lifestyle. He didn't have a good suit anymore, and he did not want to shell out the money for a suit because he and Baldy were saving for future apartment rental. He knew Sam would understand totally. And yet he couldn't help but feel a bit inferior, a feeling he didn't like having. Not because it made him feel inferior but because it meant he wasn't as satisfied as he thought he was with who he'd become. *If I'm satisfied with my life, it shouldn't matter what anyone else thinks. Should it?*

When they reached the funeral home, MacBean would not go in. He had worn a hat to partially cover his face, so no one would recognize him. Wearing clean dockers and shirt, why would anybody think he was MacBean? That guy always wore handmade Italian suits. Seeing the line snaking out the door, he turned around and left. As he did, he noted an alarm box and for a second he wondered whether or not he could pay a visit to Sam later that evening when the building was closed. *I'm smart enough to deactivate some alarms, why not? Sam would even appreciate that, I bet.*

At 10:30 P.M., MacBean returned to the now closed Fairston Funeral Home dressed in his usual hobo clothes. He held his breath, and climbed through an unlocked window and then ran to deactivate a low tech alarm system by the front door. No alarm went off.

There were three different people being waked, but it was easy to find Mr. Slade's room. Once he saw Sam, he felt a sadness mixed with great gratitude for having had this man in his life. As he continued looking at Sam's body, the thought came to him how similar in size they were, both being approximately six feet, around one hundred and ninety pounds when Sam had been healthier. With gentleness and respect MacBean took off Sam's expensive suit, shirt and tie. Then he removed his socks and shoes. Next, he put his own clothes and shoes on Sam. He knew Sam would not have minded. They had even talked about how much good food people threw away. *This isn't any different than that.* He felt even closer to Sam, in fact, once he thought he knew why he was doing this. MacBean closed the casket and left the funeral home without leaving a fingerprint. Sam's shoes were a little loose, but MacBean felt even odder being in a suit for the first time in years and he found the material of the pants felt delightfully smooth, but the structure of the jacket, shirt and tie felt like a strait jacket.

The incident turned out to be a bigger deal than MacBean had imagined. It made the national news and newspapers across the country. There was even a picture in the New York Times showing the funeral director and Slade relatives screaming when the casket was opened to find her husband dressed up in dirty jeans and a tee, plus the floppy fedora hat MacBean had worn earlier that afternoon. *Oops, got to watch out for those cameras, next time.* MacBean surprised even himself at the words "next time."

The people across the country that read newspapers or watched the evening news found this to be entertaining. But MacBean was not yet done with this caper. He also had Sam's social security number and his bank ATM number in his database file, and he wanted to use it. *How can I possibly charge something? I'd need a fake card or fake ID. How?* At that precise moment, the name Blackie popped into his head. *Blackie Blackstone, of course! I think he's out of prison by now. But how the hell do I get in touch with him? Last I heard, he was somewhere in Rhode Island.* Next day, MacBean headed to the library and looked up articles about Blackie, who had dreamed of going straight, being a car salesman, but life hadn't worked out quite like that. *He went into daddy's business after all.* MacBean found a two-year-old address and found a number in a phone book under Nicholas Blackstone, Jr. He left the library and purchased a disposable phone. With trepidation he dialed, not knowing who or what to expect.

"Hello"

"Hi, my name is JoJo MacBean. I'm an old friend of Blackie Blackstone and I'm wondering if you know how to get hold of him."

"Who is this?"

"JoJo MacBean. I grew up with Blackie and…"

"Far as I'm concerned Blackie Blackstone Senior is dead."

"Oh. You mean, really, dead I mean? Or, uh, dead to you like?"

"Dead to me. This is his son." At that news, MacBean felt an overwhelming sadness come over him.

"When your dad and I were both twelve, he told me he had two dreams. First, to be a car salesman, have no idea why. Second, to be a good dad, spend time with his son. See, his own dad never did that. And he wanted something different for his son."

"Oh really. Well, maybe he should have lived a different kind of life then, you think?!"

"Don't hang up. Please, I just want to see an old friend. I don't know what happened to your dad's dream, but I can promise you he's sad about it, I know that in my, don't laugh now, but in my heart. Please."

"How do I know you're not some other criminal, too?"

"I guess you don't. But I'm not. It's pretty clear your dad hurt you. I get that. Life hurts sometimes. But you don't stop the hurting by hurting back. It never works."

There was a silence between the two men until Blackie, Jr. quietly said, "OK, OK, I can take a chance, just don't ever call me again. I don't have a number, but he's living over a small Salvation Army store in Woonsocket, RI. He goes by the name of Blackie Nicholas now. "

"Thanks, man, really, thank you so much."

Just as MacBean was ready to press the hang up button, Blackie, Jr. said, "Wait, don't hang up. Did, did my old man really say that about wanting to be a good dad?"

"As God is my witness, son, as God is my witness." Blackie, Jr. then ended the phone call.

MacBean went back to the library for more research and finally found a number for the Salvation Army. The folks there, after many assurances that MacBean was indeed an old friend, gave him Blackie's number. When he dialed, his heart was beating quickly, and he wondered if this was the right thing to be doing.

"Hello?" Blackie answered in a voice MacBean instantly recognized.

"Blackie, I don't know if you remember. . ."

"Holy Crap, is this Mac and Beans, the genius?"

"Yes, it is. Can't believe you remember me."

"Course I do. You remember me, right? Otherwise you wouldn't be calling."

"Sorry, I let us lose touch. Especially with all that's happened, you know."

"Hey, water under the bridge. I'm happy now to be talking with you. But why now?"

"Ah, that's a long story". And so MacBean told Blackie his story about Maria and living a so-called hobo life and now stealing from a dead person. MacBean ended by asking if Blackie knew how MacBean could get a fake credit card with the info that MacBean had on a client. Blackie responded that was easy as pie. MacBean gave Blackie the numbers, and Blackie said he would express the card to the local post office the next day, but MacBean would need to go there to set up a mailbox before the card arrived. Blackie seemed genuinely glad that he could help out an old friend, and said to call him whenever he needed another card, just remember to get that short-term mailbox ahead of time. They ended the conversation promising a visit soon. MacBean could tell that Blackie needed a friend to talk to that he didn't need to keep up a false cheerful exterior with.

In the morning he signed up for the mailbox, and the card arrived in the afternoon. MacBean visited a restaurant in Valley Forge, PA the next evening where he charged about three-hundred dollars for some delicious Steak Diane with a couple of appetizers, some crème brule and a bottle of expensive champagne to boot. Back in those days, credit card companies weren't as quick to detect fraud. At the restaurant, he met a lovely lady eating by herself and asked if he could join her, picking up the tab. They had a stimulating conversation. He then escorted this lady to her apartment door where they said their goodbyes, reluctantly on both sides. He had no intention of any involvement with a woman, but it was nice to enjoy feminine company. The evening made him think of both Maria and Rivers. He was surprised to find that he missed both of them. He also figured both of them would be pleased to know he spent a *platonic* evening. He laughed when it occurred to him that the old MacBean would have married the woman! Yet he knew the lady would not have found him half so charming had they been eating at a diner.

As he left her at her door, he thought *no one is going to miss three-hundred dollars for one meal.* MacBean found Baldy waiting at the train station, where he gave him a giant bag of deli sandwiches for his own supper.

"Are you going to tell me why you're still dressed like that?"

"I will, my friend, but eat those sandwiches first, and I'll go get our ticket back to Springfield." Baldy dove into the bag, finding a Reuben, a Philly cheesesteak, and a pulled pork sandwich, along with onion rings and steak fries. On the train, MacBean filled him in on what had happened, and what MacBean was thinking about for a follow-up. MacBean also knew that charging an expensive meal would not have met with Sam's approval.

The national media continued to talk and write about Mr. Sam Slade, the prominent deceased business entrepreneur and the mysterious change of clothes. Of course, the clothes MacBean had worn were much cleaner than the average bum, but it was still a funny story to many people. People on the street were all talking and laughing about the incident. MacBean imagined the brokers on Wall Street talking around the water coolers trying to figure it out. One commentator on

TV posited that Sam Slade's ghost did it because he thought it was wasteful to be buried in such an expensive suit. *That's just what I thought!*

No one detected the meal charge at this point because the charge occurred in the beginning of a monthly cycle. But he didn't use the card again, nonetheless, to be safe. Back in West Springfield, MacBean found a homeless guy about his size and asked him if he would like a fancy suit. You should have seen the look on his face. He said that he would love it because his mother needed a good suit to bury his brother in. When MacBean heard that, he burst out laughing, inappropriately, but he couldn't help himself. Then he gave the guy the suit in a paper bag. He also made the guy swear never to tell anyone how he'd gotten it. MacBean knew the promise he'd gotten from the guy might not be worth the paper bag the suit was in, but it wouldn't surprise him either, if the man never told. *People are people – good or bad, everywhere.*

About a week later, working on a computer at a local deli, he caught a talk show on television while taking a break and eating his pay for the job. The Sam Slade topic came up, but nothing said was in any way connected to JoJo MacBean. It was at that moment he realized that what he had done was the most sheer fun of anything he'd done since Maria's death. It was the beginning of a new chapter of his life since living the hobo life – he was going to steal from dead people and give back to those who needed it. MacBean broke into four other funeral parlors across the country when former clients in his database list about his size passed away. He repeated what he'd done his first time with Sam, making a quick hit and run. The wakes and funerals for each of these clients took place in Cleveland, Seattle, D.C., and Mobile.

The funeral in Cleveland threw MacBean a curve ball. It was for a client named Sammy Charles, who had been a professional baseball player, with the nickname Sweet Sammy. He was MacBean's age and was a terrific athlete, although it hadn't prevented his early death. Although Sammy had been a Yankee fan in his youth, the closest he ever got to playing with the Yankees was when his team played the Bronx Bombers. Lonnie and MacBean had caught some of Sammy's high school games when the team made the state playoffs, and, of course, whenever Cleveland played at Yankee Stadium. In spite of not being a Yankee, he earned good money and had the savvy needed to save most of it for investing. He'd also been quite good looking and a dapper dresser, earning some endorsement money for men's clothing and watches. He was to be waked at the Farrell Funeral Home back in Cleveland, even though he'd retired back in Manhattan where he grew up. Once MacBean knew that, he was on a train to Cleveland. When he arrived the night before the wake, he decoded the alarm and entered. He was expecting to change into one of those fancy suits Sammy advertised. Much to MacBean's surprise, Sammy was dressed in his Cleveland Indians uniform and cap. He had actually ended his baseball career as an announcer for the Baltimore Orioles, but clearly his heart was always with Cleveland. MacBean thought about how he and his dad loved to see Sweet Sammy glide around the bases, stretching a double into a triple, or robbing balls hit into the gap from his center field position, like a bolt of lightning. It was a dilemma of whether to change into the uniform. *No guy cares about not being in his burial suit. But this, this is different. The man died thinking he'd be in his uniform for eternity.* MacBean tore a page out of a guest book and wrote a note that said "Thanks for the memories, Sweet Sammy, hope you don't mind too much, I borrowed your cap. I promise to be buried in it someday, so I can give it back to you!" MacBean took off the baseball cap but had nothing to replace it with. So, he made a paper hat with some more paper, placed that on the man's head and put the note on top of his folded hands. But MacBean smiled to himself every time he thought about what the reaction would have been if he'd given the uniform to a homeless man. But he knew he'd done the right thing. He also knew that a younger MacBean would not have understood the choice.

At the other three funeral homes, he switched clothes with the deceased. And at all four, he accessed their card numbers, bought a disposable phone to call Blackie with the card info and then picked it up at the mailbox he'd already set up. Just to be on the safe side, he'd also gotten a new ID with the name MacDyer on it, using his original birth certificate, just so no one in the future could connect the mailbox with MacBean. He would also give the suit away the next day to someone who needed it. But instead of having a good meal himself, he used the cards to order pizzas and calzones for delivery to a food kitchen in the area for the next six days, and he purchased hundreds of coffee shop and deli gift cards that he literally handed to every person in that city or town who looked like they needed one. *Sure, some guys would sell the cards for booze or drugs, but some wouldn't.* He also gave some to the food kitchen to give out to those they felt were least likely to sell them. And he always capped the total charge at around that three-hundred-dollar mark, enough to make a difference to people in need, but not enough to draw much attention. MacBean's only worry was that he would make a card with an invalid number. Some people cancelled a card of a deceased person fairly quickly, others waited until the fog of grief cleared their mind, and still others had joint cards so that the remaining spouse's card was still valid. MacBean figured the odds were with him, the same way he'd always figured the odds were with his stock choices. It became a game to him, a game he began to enjoy thoroughly, giving him the same kind of rush a good stock tip had, even though Baldy was always urging him to "make this one the last one, MacBean, the odds are gonna catch up with you, man." But MacBean knew that Baldy was enjoying the game, too. It was Baldy who suggested he tag along to keep an eye out, outside, for anyone showing up unexpectedly. MacBean could see the gleam in Baldy's eyes, and he could feel his bear hug of congratulations growing stronger after leaving each funeral home.

Of course, the news media were all over these stories, and viewers and readers were definitely entertained. The "hobo ghost" was the hottest topic in any conversations that came up throughout the country. There were three more switches early in 2006, in Baton Rouge, Miami, and Savannah, making the total then to eight. All had been successful with no traces of evidence. Even if someone discovered the unexplained charges, there was nothing directly connecting that to the funeral home events and no way to connect any of it to MacBean.

A little fly don't need a shotgun shell.
– Detective Kline.

Even though he had harmed no one, funeral homes were getting a little antsy. If someone found it that easy to break into their building, what else might they do once inside, such as steal a body itself? The time was reached when somebody would have to be put in charge of catching him, even though there was no clue at that point about who committed these crimes. As they occurred in multiple states, the FBI took on the case. The agency asked retired New York City detective Ronald A. Kline II to consult on the case because Kline had an expertise in nonviolent serial crimes and had solved a case in the early nineties around several break-ins of Seven Elevens during which a couple Slurpee's were made and a bag of mini, powdered donuts was taken. Never the cigarettes, never the beer, just Slurpee's and only the one bag of donuts. Kline had figured out that this was a crime by someone who thought he was smarter than law enforcement. For two years, he was right. Then Kline came on board and figured out who it was from the details of the first break-in. That Seven Eleven had been scheduled for closing, and the store manager was angry at corporate for doing that. In talking to other employees in that store, he discovered that the manager loved those little white donuts in the bag. Once he discovered that manager had disappeared after that first break-in, Kline knew he'd found his man. He circulated the man's face to every Seven Eleven in the country and on the TV channels in the cities and towns with Seven Elevens. The manager was caught literally eating the evidence one night just a few blocks from a break-in in Detroit. Only Kline took the time to think about the motive instead of rounding up all the petty criminals in each city every time a break-in had occurred. The manager told Kline, "I just didn't know what else a guy like me could do. Hey, you want a donut?" Kline still remembered sharing a donut with a man with powdered sugar all around his lips, and how the two of them laughed when Kline bit into his donut and the white powder fell all over his suit jacket. He also told the judge that if all his cases had involved that kind of white powder, many lives would have been saved. The manager spent just a few months in jail before being granted probation of a couple years. Kline even helped the man get into a trainee program for bakers. Last year, the manager sent the detective a box of donuts the man had made from scratch, thanking Kline for catching him. Kline's wife wouldn't let him eat the donuts because of his diabetes, but he snuck one late at night and was not surprised it was the best tasting Boston crème he'd ever had.

Later in 2006, Detective Kline started studying the facts about the eight-funeral parlor break-ins. It did not take him long to start asking the right question: is there something these men of extreme wealth had in common, perhaps something related to their wealth that made them a target?

Kline began by reviewing the assets held by each of the deceased men. He noticed that in each case, most of the assets were held under a company called Kurtzner Brothers Limited. He met with the KBL security team and asked who would have had access to a client list, now or in the recent past, and were there any employees with such access who had been fired or left under less than happy circumstances in the past few years? One name popped up, even though everyone at KBL told him that MacBean was an honest man, a straight arrow almost to a fault. But Kline knew better, the Seven Eleven employees had said the same thing about their store manager. Of course, the KBL security and brokers were embarrassed and didn't want any of their clients to know they'd been careless with a clients' list.

Kline also caught on to the credit card charges occurring a day or two after a clothes switch. He figured out MacBean had made fake cards and then destroyed them after running up approximately three-hundred dollars each time. What he didn't yet know was why these particular food charges, but he did suspect there was more to the story, since the charges were never for anything other than food – so much food, in fact, no single man could eat it.

Since the thefts, individually, were considered minor, Kline decided to not yet make his discovery public to either the FBI or the media so that MacBean would not be tipped off. In fact, Kline felt sure that MacBean would soon tire of his capers and that would be the end of it. So, he decided to keep what he'd found to himself a while longer and to go undercover to find MacBean and end it one way or another. He also knew that KBL would not let the theft of a client list pass by unnoticed. If he could persuade MacBean to give himself up, perhaps public pressure would lessen KBL's wrath.

The entire country continued to enjoy hearing about the break-ins when they occurred. Since every time period always had plenty of depressing news, the break-ins provided a welcome light moment in the news. This little humor that MacBean provided was a positive note for many throughout the country.

Once KBL gave Detective Kline a list of the clientele

that MacBean had serviced during his years at the brokerage firm, he figured he would keep track of the list and stay on top of any former clients who died. If he could try to get to the funeral parlor where the deceased would be waked before MacBean did, he'd have a chance to catch him red handed.

KLINE MEETS SKILLET, SKILLET WINS

Very late in 2006, just before MacBean's sixtieth birthday, another former client passed away. He was sorry to read about "Big Bucks" Fulham III. Detective Kline immediately knew that Big Bucks was on his client list, and he flew to the Adams Funeral Parlor in San Diego, where Big Bucks was to be waked. Kline got there before MacBean because MacBean never showed up. Big Bucks weighed almost four hundred pounds, over twice MacBean's weight. Kline knew the connection between MacBean's switches and size of the dead client, but he didn't want to take the chance that MacBean would come up with some other way to involve the former client.

A few more weeks went by, and another one of MacBean's former clients passed away. It was none other than the B-movie actor Dipsey Doolittle. This was all over the news as Dipsey was not that old but died filming a love scene in a spaghetti western. Everybody joked that he died in the saddle. Although relatively young, most agreed if your number's up, not a bad way to go. When MacBean got a newspaper the next day, he read that Dipsey would be cremated and that it was a private funeral for family only. At KBL everyone liked Dipsey and thought he was quite the character. Seeing as Dipsey was being cremated, MacBean had no reason to go near where he was being waked. *Happy trails, pardner.*

Then another month went by, and another former client, Arnold A. Horvath, passed away and he was about MacBean's size. Horvath was to be waked at his place of birth in Biloxi, Mississippi, even though he had spent his entire career and retirement in NYC. MacBean had, just the day before, completed programming his database to notify him if any client similar in size with an obituary in the client's hometown newspaper passed away. That day Baldy and he were at a San Antonio clinic because Baldy wasn't feeling well, when MacBean heard the "bing" of his computer alerting him to Arnold's passing. *What luck, I'm near Biloxi.* Of course, Detective Kline had received his own "bing", but MacBean didn't know that as yet.

Kline set up a plan at the Biloxi Funeral Home to catch MacBean in the act. Kline figured that he would lie in a casket in the room next to Horvath and wait patiently for MacBean's break-in.

The owner of the funeral home, Mr. Joshua Ledemeyer, was a wealthy man in his own right. Joshua had been having an affair with a much younger mistress for several years. As it turned out, this young mistress was on the payroll as a cleaning lady. MacBean surmised she was undoubtedly well-paid for both her services. The night before the wake, the detective laid down in the casket.

It was around 9 P.M., and there were no other wakes at the funeral home. The real Horvath was to be waked the next evening. As MacBean attempted to gain entrance, he realized to his surprise that the alarm was not on. MacBean just figured Mr. Ledemeyer, busy with "other" things, had simply forgotten to set it.

But Mr. Ledemeyer had imbibed a few drinks and also forgot that detective Kline was lying in a casket hoping that MacBean would break-in that evening. Kline was all dressed up in a nice suit, trying to lay as still as the aches and pains of age would let him. MacBean quietly entered the building and quickly realized that Ledemeyer and his mistress were carrying out their hot and steamy sexual affair in a room next to Kline. Detective Kline could see the shadows on the wall of the two lovers while the couple were engaged. He heard them screaming in blissful delight. The young lady was scantily clad in a black see-through negligee, and she was really moaning. Kline, though in his late sixties, couldn't help becoming aroused. When the sex was over, the scantily dressed couple cleaned up, put on their clothes, then left the building, with Ledemeyer forgetting altogether that Kline was there. MacBean had observed nearly the entire sex scene but remained quiet, still unaware of Kline's presence. MacBean saw Ledemeyer set the alarm, which he duly noted, and which MacBean quickly turned off after Ledemeyer left the building.

Detective Kline was about the size of MacBean. As he approached the casket quietly, MacBean could easily see that it was someone else in the casket. The name of the deceased was not on the billboard yet. Kline's eyes were shut but something told MacBean that this guy didn't look dead, and he could see a faint rising and falling of the chest. MacBean figured it was a set up. All he needed was the confirmation from the man in the casket that was provided by Kline's woody pitching a tent after that steamy sex scene. MacBean snuck into a small kitchen at the funeral home and grabbed a heavy fry pan. He then again quietly snuck up to Kline's casket. A spur of the moment reaction made him bop Kline's crotch as hard as he could. With Kline screaming, MacBean rushed out of the funeral home as fast as he could, whispering as loud as he dared, "Baldy, scram."

Detective Kline was hospitalized for a few days, but incapacitated for several weeks, eventually going on semi-permanent disability. The great detective was totally embarrassed and was never so humiliated in his life. Of course, when this story hit the papers nationally, it was greeted with hilarity by readers. All the newscasters on TV had a ball with it. With all the bad news out there, people found this story as humorous as the funeral ghost's previous escapades. Even though MacBean left the funeral home right after the incident, he knew better than to mess with the body of Mr. Horvath. He knew there would be more than enough funerals of former clients, since most of them had been several years older than he when he was at KBL, making some quite elderly by now.

At the funeral home, however, a security camera MacBean hadn't seen captured the picture of a man looking like a homeless guy and wearing dark glasses and a hat, but his face wasn't recognizable. His hat was a gift from Baldy, and it said "Hobo JJM" on it. MacBean still had, as yet, no idea that Kline knew who he was. The media now referred to him as Hobo JJM. And everyone was asking, "Who is Hobo JJM, and what do the initials stand for?" As MacBean circulated around the country, he realized that he'd become famous again! But this time, it wasn't as the Wall Street wizard but as one of a kind, exclusive character. He wondered whether nonviolent criminals ever made it to the top ten most wanted list. Kline had decided to play his cards close to his vest and still kept quiet about the identify of Hobo JJM, at least while he figured out who to get to help him with the case now that he could do little physical exertion for a while.

The authorities knew that Hobo JJM could be anywhere at any time. These policemen were told by their superiors that if they came across him, they should handle carefully because the general public was now rooting for him not to get caught. After all, he was stealing from men who could well afford it. And this was before it became public about what MacBean did with the bogus credit cards.

Every day that went by, MacBean was the topic of conversation not only in the USA, but all over the world. Whether it was local bars, gyms, at the workplace or on TV, he was the light moment that people needed in their stressful world. MacBean couldn't figure out why it was so; he only knew it was – that he enjoyed his fame as Hobo JJM more than he ever did his pinnacle of success on Wall Street. He was eating decent meals, still assembling computers for a few bucks and reading books, periodicals and newspapers, so he could continue giving deli owners throughout the country stock tips in exchange for food. It was an adventurous life! MacBean felt as happy as he ever remembered feeling after childhood and close to his happiness with Maria.

The deli owners, whom MacBean had helped with computer help or stock tips, had decided to a man to keep MacBean from getting caught. It had begun when one of the early deli owners named Karl Steuben, known for his famous "Steuben Reuben", helped spread the word through a regional association of deli owners that if they encountered MacBean they could trust him and would be well rewarded for that trust. From there, the word spread nationally to other deli owners. A few others, such as Giorgio Minelli and Aaron Moses, were particularly good at finding ways to get MacBean updated parts he needed, not only for their own deli computer needs, but with software that MacBean could install and take with him on his own computer. When he unthinkingly wore his Hobo JJM hat into a local deli in Schenectady, the owner protected him by knocking it off his head to which MacBean said, "Thanks, I must have left my brain in my other hat." Some deli owners even contacted their friends and colleagues across the country, who also owned delis or other businesses, to alert them that MacBean was one of the good guys, and you'd be lucky if he stopped by. And they even began to share stock tips with one another. So MacBean kept on moving from one destination to another, many thanks to those deli owners. Deli owners that hadn't had a visit began to feel cheated! MacBean had become, yet again, an A list celebrity. Yet not a single deli owner didn't also wonder about the circumstances that drove MacBean from Wall Street to no street.

There was still no stress or major concerns in MacBean's

life since he had no idea Kline knew who he was. It seemed to MacBean to be important to him that this was so. The time he spent with other homeless throughout the country was an experience that he knew was far more important to him than any "killing" he ever made on Wall Street. He told his stories to them in hopes it could inspire them in some small way, the same way that their stories continued to inspire him. Very few of his homeless friends knew that he was the Hobo JJM, and he never stayed around for more than a week or two at a time. MacBean had become quite the drifter as it felt the safest way to be. But there was one thing different in this life that MacBean recognized as something he never wanted to be without again. That was a friend as good as Baldy. He wasn't just a traveling companion. Baldy wasn't just the logistics part of their team, helping figure out something that MacBean didn't know about this lifestyle. The man held MacBean when he found himself overcome with regrets and sadness. Baldy gave him the necessary pep talk when MacBean was nervous about what the future could bring. Baldy was the one to smack him down a peg or two when he started to get too full of himself. Baldy always did that by handing MacBean a roll of toilet paper, just like Abraham had done once. And Baldy was the one who understood how lonely life was for some people, whether they were big shots on Wall Street or bums on skid row. MacBean had started calling him "brother Baldy". Most people thought it was just a riff on "bro" or just a nickname. But Baldy knew full well that MacBean meant it as a way to tell him that he had become as beloved as a brother would be, that he'd become MacBean's brother in all but name.

The funeral parlor break-ins continued into 2007 when a former client about the right size finally passed away. The exchange of wardrobes with his deceased former clientele, and the pizzas and food charged on credit, continued. In fact, MacBean did two such "hit and runs" since the Kline incident. The elegant suit from each caper was eventually given to another homeless man that MacBean never met, so the police would only hear the truth, i.e. "I don't know the guy; he just handed me the suit." Naturally, such a dressed up homeless guy did attract attention, but MacBean usually handed it to them at night, so he could be out of town by the time anyone saw the odd sight. He even had the local police chuckling when they'd see someone they recognized in a fancy suit, as word had spread throughout police departments to be on the look- out for such things. In each case, the policeman would question the newly dressed up homeless man, and nothing much came out of it because the guy really couldn't see well who had given it to him. MacBean's legend continued to grow as Hobo JJM. Ever the businessman, MacBean even thought about finding a way to order caps made with "Hobo JJM" on them and handing them out for free to every homeless guy he could. That would drive police and the FBI nuts. Eventually, he might sell them to the non-homeless as novelty items.

Finally, in early 2007, Detective Kline felt able to go back to the hunt and told the FBI that he'd figured out it was Joseph Joshua MacBean. The FBI had accused the detective of knowing all along but not wanting anybody else to "solve" the case. Of course, Kline denied that but felt justified in having done so because he was not about to let some Wall Street punk do what MacBean had done to him without personally bringing him to justice. At that point, the FBI froze MacBean's accounts. When he attempted to get some cash from an ATM and his card was declined, MacBean knew they were closing in. He wasn't worried about the cash; he was earning enough from his computer and stock tip businesses to cover his basic needs. But he was worried that the life of freedom he'd come to treasure might end sooner than he'd have chosen.

The media splashed it across headlines nationally – JoJo MacBean, former KBL wunderkind and genius, was suspected as the funeral home ghost and Hobo JJM. It was Rivers Fitzpatrick who visited the FBI and told them to track just where and what the credit card charges had purchased. She was sure there would be a pattern of some kind for she had faith in MacBean as having learned something along his travels. When they discovered the pattern that pizza joints and food kitchens benefitted most from the charges, that, too, was splashed all over the headlines.

MacBean not only enjoyed each caper, he thrived on them. As several editorials had pointed out, "Who was Hobo JJM hurting?" None of the widows of his former deceased clients expressed any taste for going after him. The widows never pressed any charges because a stolen suit and some credit card charges were minor to them. Now that they knew who he was, they knew full well that he had made their families many thousands of dollars, even millions, and MacBean felt it was likely that most of these widows felt sorry for him. What no one but Baldy knew was that MacBean was having great fun.

SMURTZ MEETS GAS, GAS WINS

By the end of 2007, and MacBean nearing sixty-one, there had been over twenty funeral parlor break-ins around the country. He had never felt more alive or more filled with purpose. He still often thought of Maria, usually just before falling asleep. When he woke in the morning, he found himself thinking of Rivers. Maria loved him in spite of his faults, but he was sure Rivers loved him because of who he was becoming. He was also sure he would never tell Rivers how he felt about her because he was not yet ready to risk such pain again.

Police forces all over the country were now on the alert for MacBean. Detective Kline asked a fellow associate, from Saint Paul, Minnesota, named Fred Smurtz to join him on the case. Kline figured he needed somebody to help with the physical aspects of capturing MacBean, since Kline couldn't help but feel terror at the thought of being close enough to MacBean for another big bop. Smurtz was also retired, and when Kline called him about this case, Smurtz had initially replied, "No way" and then hung up the phone on Kline, who immediately called back.

"Hear me out, let me come see you in Minnesota and bend your ear for a couple of hours."

"If I say 'no', you're still gonna come, aren't you?" asked Smurtz.

Kline then hopped on a plane to Minnesota and told him about how he became partially disabled a couple of years ago. Smurtz was trying not to chuckle, but he couldn't stop himself. "Oh yeah!" Smurtz replied, "I seem to have heard something about that!" But Smurtz also admitted that this was an interesting case.

Kline then asked Smurtz to consider coming out of retirement because he was the finest detective out there that he knew. Smurtz promised Kline that he would give this situation some thought.

Two weeks later, Smurtz called Kline and said that he was up for the challenge. It would be a nice final chapter in his career if he could catch MacBean, alias Hobo JJM. Smurtz told Kline that he just hoped his skills were good enough to handle one final case. Smurtz also said "No man, no matter what his motives, is above the law. NO MAN."

Detective Smurtz was confident he could help solve this case. Although seventy-five years old, he still had the mind of a young Eliot Ness. He was far from a high-tech guy, but he had a one hundred percent capture and convict record during his career, something few other detectives could claim. Kline being one of those others, Smurtz knew Kline would be as motivated as he was to bring MacBean to justice.

Smurtz was every bit a "hard ass," but he was also wise enough to know that JJM was not violent. Truth be told, Smurtz felt his retirement was not all he'd hoped for, in fact he was quite bored much of the time. He had lost his wife and his best friend in the same week, shortly after he retired. Smurtz had gone to his wife's grave practically every day until Kline got him to accept this assignment. Now he spent his time with Kline learning all he could about MacBean.

Kline had researched MacBean's life and reviewed all of the details from childhood to the present with Smurtz. Kline then went over the client list at Kurtzner Brothers Limited, indicating which clients were deceased and which were living. He also reviewed the clients most like MacBean's size, especially the older ones with more risk of dying. Smurtz then visited Kurtzner Brothers Limited and the executives at Triton, talking to them about working with MacBean, gathering any facts he could. He'd figure out if they were important or not later on.

But what Smurtz found was that the information he had obtained didn't really help that much because MacBean's coworkers really didn't know him that well on a personal level. MacBean had been all business all the time. He figured that MacBean was still all business in a different way now. He discovered that MacBean had no relatives who knew him and very few friends except for the woman with the funny Irish name who had helped the FBI figure out MacBean's motive.

Smurtz wrote in his notes that MacBean was a workaholic, a high-tech guru, and a Harvard dropout that was bored with the classroom, even though he had terrific grades. MacBean was the nerdy type, a very intelligent human being, but a total failure in marriage. He interviewed MacBean's first three wives and concluded they really didn't know him either. After all, they hadn't spent much time with him or vice versa. Smurtz also learned about MacBean's marriage to Maria Fontana and the tragic ending to her life. It was evident that MacBean had been very happy with Maria and had begun to better balance his work and personal life even to the detriment of making more money. Smurtz even flew to Italy to meet with Maria's parents to see if they could provide any more information about him, but that long trip did not lead to anything more to help his case.

Smurtz was not without some degree of sympathy for MacBean. But he was nonetheless determined to be the man who caught the Wall Street hobo. Fred Smurtz knew that this might be the toughest case of his career because so many people didn't want to see MacBean caught. He also knew that MacBean was a very smart man but not a thug or worse. Finally, it dawned on him – *Kline's not the only one that can play pretend.*

Shortly after Smurtz started this case, another former wealthy client on MacBean's KBL client list died in Port Orange, Florida by the name of Donald O. Katz. Katz had a brilliant career although he never personally owned a company. He'd been the CEO of two Fortune 500 companies. He was also the most disagreeable, unforgiving, selfish man MacBean had ever met. A meeting with Katz meant conversations about the faults of every human being except Katz. His specialty was blatant misogyny. There wasn't a broker at KBL who did not despise the man.

When MacBean broke into the funeral parlor in Port Orange the night before the wake to exchange wardrobes with the dead man, he'd come up with a twist. He had gone to a consignment shop and picked out a glitzy, gauzy pink and rhinestone dress and dressed Katz in it and then added lipstick and cheek blush. When that coffin was opened, unlike the usual shock, the family roared a sense of relief that the old man had finally gotten his comeuppance, even if a little late. In fact, they didn't bother to change him for the wake, a fact which the media picked up, and which further bolstered the comedic aspect of the capers. Per usual MacBean picked up his fake charge card in Katz's name and proceeded to charge food and café gift cards about an hour away in Ocala, as well as giving the man's suit to a homeless guy.

Before making a beeline out of Florida, MacBean sensed that the people chasing him had fully caught on to what he was doing. He knew he needed to move quicker than ever before. Finding a bum to exchange clothes with wasn't difficult, and it still gave the police a laugh when they discovered a street guy in a fancy suit. MacBean continued to keep the charges to under three hundred dollars, literally like pennies to his former clients. And he began to be even more careful about leaving any trails. After six months trying to find a trail, Smurtz decided to call the retired Detective Kline to see if he was willing to keep track of the remaining former clients, which were about MacBean's size, on a daily basis, perhaps even hourly. Smurtz settled for asking Kline for a twice daily update on anything happening out of the normal. He knew that Kline had better tech skills and could extract the right information from the database that Kline had built, a database eerily similar to the one MacBean had made. Kline told Smurtz that he would do his best on this and would contact all the clients and tell them to make sure their families notified Kline if anything happened to that particular client. MacBean suspected some of his former clients ignored Kline's request, knowing that MacBean was essentially harmless. In fact, MacBean was sure a few of them probably thought he'd simply lost his mind. It made MacBean grateful that some of them might still have a sense of loyalty to him due to his past service and also knowing MacBean's sad history in his last year with KBL.

It was early 2008 and, although he was still pretty nimble and able to move around at a quick pace, MacBean was beginning to question how much longer he could do this and escape capture.

Smurtz had, in fact, gotten a notification from Kline about another of MacBean's clients passing away. His name was Milton E. Noyes from Palo Alto, California. Noyes was a lifelong bachelor with no remaining family. Kline also told Smurtz that Milton was indeed similar size to MacBean. The Filton Funeral Home, where Noyes was to be waked, received the call from Fred Smurtz. Mr. Joseph Filton, the owner of the funeral home, happened to be there at the time of the phone call. Detective Smurtz gave Filton the rundown. He asked Filton if he could delay the wake one more day. It was the perfect case because Milton had no family. Mr. Filton didn't have to worry about pleasing any relatives of the deceased and agreed to do so.

Smurtz then proceeded to hire one of the best make-up artists to try to make him look like Milton E. Noyes. The night before the wake, Smurtz slipped into the casket wearing a designer suit. The funeral parlor was closed, and a couple dim lights were on.

As MacBean slipped into the Filton Funeral after disarming the alarm, he entered the place cautiously, unaware that detective Smurtz had figured out MacBean's next move. But Smurtz must have gotten overly excited, or had an especially big supper, because he blew his cover with as big a fart as MacBean had ever heard, when he entered the room!

MacBean fled the place like a bat out of hell! *You almost had me, but you blew it in more ways than one!* That was the first time Smurtz thought maybe he wasn't up to undercover work anymore.

When MacBean left Filton Funeral Home, he and Baldy, waiting for him outside, didn't stop running for three miles. When they finally stopped, it was with a simultaneous sigh of relief and a gasping for breath. *Crap, my future was dependent on a fart.* He didn't call Blackie for a card, and they left town on the first train they could get, not caring where it was headed. It wasn't until they were safely on the train that MacBean told Baldy the whole story. Baldy still hadn't fully caught his breath from the running. As the two men sat in their seats trying not to attract attention, bouts of gasping and laughing overtook them several times before they each finally fell asleep. But before sleep overcame him, MacBean thought to himself, *Now that the FBI knows it's me, what comes next?* MacBean actually chuckled as he understood that he was essentially trapped. *All the more reason to play it out to the very end, have as much fun as I can before the game is over.* When the train had gone at least one hundred miles, they deboarded and located a computer in the library to send an email to Rivers on a newly set up Gmail account. MacBean could only hope that Rivers would know who "SamFriend@gmail.com" was. He wrote only "Having a wonderful time. Game's almost over". As they looked for a place to rest a while, Baldy seemed pensive.

"I thought you were in high spirits from that disaster," said MacBean.

"I haven't laughed that hard since, well, I don't know since when."

"So why the sad face, my friend?"

"I have to tell you something, something you don't want to hear."

"It's time, isn't it?"

"I can't go on, MacBean. I mean I want to, but I can't."

"Why the hell didn't you tell me?"

"You know damned well the two of us been playing pretend, not wanting the other to worry about what the future'll bring. And I been feeling better than I ever thought I could."

"But that's why you should have told me! I'm your friend. Hell, you're probably the best friend I've ever had. You should, aw shit, this is awful."

"Do you know I've never heard you say "shit" before. You must really care" said Archie with a smile on his face, looking to MacBean for acceptance of the inevitable.

"Are you sure? I mean, I can find specialists you know, I still got some connections."

"No, I'm not lying. When I ran from the funeral home, I thought I was gonna die right there, right then. My lungs were burning, I felt like vomiting, I thought it was the end."

"I should have known that. Sorry, man. I wasn't thinking, like the old MacBean."

"You ain't the old MacBean."

"So, what are we going to do?"

"We aren't going to do anything, MacBean. I am going to try and get into the VA in Holyoke, Mass. I know they all have waiting lists, but, you know, after all, I'm dying, maybe that matters, maybe it doesn't. I'll find out."

"You'll get in, or they will never hear the end of it from JoJo MacBean, I promise you that!"

The next morning, they boarded another train, and then, after a couple rides from truck drivers, they reached the VA Hospital where Baldy was admitted. An email sent to Rivers, who contacted her father, who knew people in D.C., made sure that Baldy got his bed. MacBean was angry it took such intervention, but he was still glad it worked. Once settled into his room, MacBean was allowed to visit Baldy.

"Are you sure about this? I bet I could get you a room in a swank hospice somewhere. You sure about. . ."

But Baldy interrupted MacBean, "I'm with my fellow vets,

man, I can't think of a better place to die than right alongside them, right along with them. I bet when we get to St. Peter's gates, there's some general waiting for us, expecting us to stand tall and proud, and say "yes, sir" and "no, sir" and telling us to "fall in line." I'd like that, hope it's true. Guess I'll find out."

MacBean stood looking at his friend. "You remind me of Sam Slade. When I saw him last, he seemed at peace, too. How does someone get that way? Sam had his foundation and knew that it would still be helping people long after he was gone. But, Baldy how can you be so resigned to this?"

"For one reason and one reason only – JoJo MacBean."

"I don't understand".

"I met you, and you met me, *for a reason.* You and I don't know yet exactly what that reason is, but someday you will. I know that in my very bones, MacBean, I feel it. There's a reason for everything, we just have to be patient in finding it out. Now get going."

"I'm not going to leave you. I'll be with you, until, you know."

"But that's what I'm telling you. I love you, man, but right now, I don't need you. I have my fellow vets to keep me company, to send me off. You need to stay on MacBean's journey, not wait around for mine to end. Go find that reason."

MacBean shook his head feeling that this was a man with a wisdom he had never fully appreciated before. He gave him a bear hug that was returned. And then MacBean scrounged around in his backpack and pulled out the small hand-made wooden cross that Jesús had made for him.

"You still have that?" asked Baldy. "Figured it was stolen with the backpack."

"It was just luck that I had it in my pocket when we were robbed. It always reminded me of other men who deserved to be remembered. And that other men had far greater burdens to bear in life than I ever had. But I want you to keep it now."

"But they'll just throw it away after I go."

"That's OK; it's done its job for me. Now it will remind you that JoJo MacBean calls you his friend and brother and that someday, God willing, we'll meet again." Baldy took the cross from MacBean's hand and held it tightly in his own. MacBean turned and left the room quickly, wiping his eyes.

Meanwhile, Detective Smurtz was now beginning to wonder if he would ever have as good a chance again as he'd had that night. He told Kline the truth about Filton Funeral Home and was glad he did, as the two old men laughed harder than they had in quite a while. Now the two detectives thought about how they could catch MacBean in another way. Even though Kline suggested Smurtz's plan had been a good one, and well worth another try as long as some Gas-X preceded Smurtz climbing into the casket, Smurtz felt that MacBean would be a lot more wary coming into a waking room and would be listening for even the softest of noises. Little did Smurtz know that it would take a while before he had another chance to catch the man. MacBean laid low for a while, as he drifted throughout the country giving stock tips to deli owners and assembling computers with discarded parts. He found he could make ends meet but that he missed the excitement of funeral home action. And he missed sharing it all with Baldy.

2008 marked the Financial crisis (preceded by both a banking and a housing crisis) resulting in the Great Recession. Housing prices fell over 30% and unemployment reached 9%. [24]

A PLAN IS HATCHED BY OUR MERRY BAND OF MEN

In mid-2008, it was time to start up again. Since MacBean was already known to everyone through the media, his audience waited for his next venture. MacBean had become, in fact, somewhat of a working person's hero. People were rooting for him not to get caught. Articles about him were entertaining to the general public throughout the world. His picture had appeared in several papers showing him during his Wall Street genius career, and drawings of what they thought he might look like as a bum frequently appeared. There were no actual pictures of him as a hobo because MacBean had done his best to hide his face from any security cameras at the funeral homes. He had, by now, officially entered "folk hero" status. Stories about his life and career and the various break-ins were being read all over the world. Some papers even ran a daily "Hobo JoJo update". Once he had been identified, the media had begun using "JoJo" because it sounded good with "hobo". Every time MacBean saw it in print, he remembered his parents fondly, they and Maria being the only ones who called him by that name. Some of the sketches were pretty amusing, many of them done by police artists estimating what he would look like at his age. A few were unsettlingly close.

Most of the homeless he met in his travels didn't connect him to "Hobo JoJo". Most of them had no idea about the funeral home break-ins. None of them knew about his former lifestyle involving "high society". He had stopped telling his life stories by that point, trying to lay low and conduct his funeral home "business". Most of the homeless lived day-to-day, some drowning their pain or their mental illness with alcohol or drugs. That never meant he wouldn't meet quite a few still able to converse well in their lucid moments. And there were always a few who were homeless due to medical bankruptcies or condition that would come and go, like PTSD or mania.

The deli owners throughout the country continued to protect MacBean. When police questioned them, even if they had met him, they never gave the police any information other than, "Yes, he was here". Like the rest of the country, they knew he was committing no real harm. Besides, their personal portfolios were "cooking" because of MacBean's stock tips.

In late 2008, MacBean added a twist to his break-ins. He started stealing the suits of other wealthy deceased people in addition to the KBL former clients. He would get their names from obituaries, saying they were being waked at the same home as the KBL clients, and MacBean would do some quick research to determine they were likely to also have quality suits. He brought in clothes he'd taken out of donation bins to redress the men. He had initially done it to confuse Smurtz. But when MacBean saw five homeless guys dressed in the suits he'd just given them, it occurred to him that it would make for great copy. He took a photo of them with the cell phone one of them had stolen and sent it to the local newspaper. The next day, that photo of five bums in impeccable suits, shirts, and ties ran across the country with headlines of different ilk. MacBean's favorite was "the Hobo JoJo Gang" but he also liked "the new board of KBL?"

The things MacBean saw during the break-ins were sometimes comical. Most funeral home directors were good, upstanding citizens. But some, as in any other profession, were out and out perverts. In some little private rooms, there were nude pictures of women, and even once in a while nude men. Of course, these little offices were locked up, so no other employees knew about them. MacBean found himself wondering if their spouses knew about the offices. Other owners had drinking or gambling problems, and, of course, a few of them had mistresses. One time an owner of a funeral home caught him in his funeral parlor browsing around when he came back after it was closing time. The man was about to call the cops, but MacBean told him he would tell his family that he was a pervert and that he had some of the man's pictures of underage girls to prove it. He was bluffing about the pictures, but the man was shaking so much MacBean knew he'd hit a nerve. Of course, the man had to let MacBean go.

During that year, MacBean had a passport doctored up and traveled to Europe to pull off his routine twice with deceased clients on his list. The added publicity on these two break-ins that occurred in Aosta, Italy and Barcelona, added to the adventure and to MacBean's sense of playing a game. It was as though he'd become a modern-day Robin Hood.

Smurtz was getting tired and running out of time. It didn't help that no one wanted to see MacBean get caught, including the families of the deceased KBL clients and deli owners. Detective Kline did his best to assist his buddy, Smurtz, about when he thought Hobo JoJo would strike next, but they kept striking out.

Smurtz then came up with another great idea. He decided to contact one of the former clients that was about the same size as MacBean. His name was Charlie I. Walker. Walker owned a conglomerate of convenience stores, gas stations, and burger joints throughout the southwest. Smurtz informed Walker about how he wanted to catch MacBean. Of course, Walker had been following the news about MacBean all along. When Smurtz asked Charlie if he could fake Charlie's death, the detective tried to convince Walker that MacBean needed to be caught before any real harm came to him. Smurtz also stressed that stealing a client list from KBL might not have ramifications now, but there was no telling what might happen to that list if it ever ended up in the wrong hands, accidentally. Walker wasn't sure he was doing what was right, but he decided to side with the law, in the hopes that he was saving MacBean from possible future harm.

A couple of weeks later the papers printed that the well-known business tycoon Charlie I. Walker was accidentally shot on a hunting expedition for wild boar near Austin, Texas. The papers had stated that a private wake for invited only would be held at the Besloe Funeral Home in Round Rock, Texas, Walker's hometown.

As MacBean headed from Knoxville, Tennessee to Round Rock by train and by hitching rides, he had no idea he was being lured into a trap.

Detective Smurtz again hired a makeup artist, but this time the makeup was applied on a younger detective named Richie Hobbs, thirty-five years old. Smurtz did not want any police involved because he knew that the fewer people who knew about this attempt, the better his chances were of catching MacBean. Smurtz asked Kline to fly in and assist him along with Detective Hobbs and a couple of other young detectives. Smurtz wanted every side of the funeral home covered. Smurtz was older than MacBean, so reinforcements with younger men only made sense to Smurtz.

Something new had been added to the hunt. KBL had become a laughing stock when picture of the five guys in new suits had been labeled in print and social media as the new board of KBL. MacBean's joke had backfired on him. A new KBL head honcho wasn't about to let the laughing continue, so the firm was now offering a reward of two hundred thousand dollars. Smurtz was fearing that bounty hunters would now enter into the hunt, especially since it seemed obvious that Hobo JoJo posed no physical threat, easy pickings in other words. Smurtz, Kline, and Walker all knew it was becoming increasingly in MacBean's best interests to get caught.

Smurtz didn't care about the reward, of course, since he'd started his hunt, as did Kline, way before any reward. Besides, they'd been at least initially hired by the FBI, so any reward would be returned to the agency. The two detectives just wanted to prove to the world that they could still "get their man" regardless of their age. However, nothing stopped the two men from wishing KBL had just hired them in the first place.

As MacBean approached the funeral parlor the night before Charlie Walker's wake, he didn't notice anything different from his previous escapades. He disarmed the alarm and went into the room assigned to Walker. Young Detective Hobbs certainly looked like old Charlie. As MacBean entered into the room, all the lights came on immediately, and Smurtz and the two other young detectives stood pointing guns at MacBean. Detective Kline came into the room without a gun but instead with a glare that could have melted an iceberg.

"Can't say I didn't have a good run." said MacBean to the detectives. Smurtz then handcuffed him per protocol. Smurtz told Hobbs and the other two young men not to mention anything to anyone about this capture until they heard back from him. He told them they'd get ten thousand each. The young men weren't FBI, so Smurtz was hoping KBL could afford to be generous since they wouldn't have to shell out the whole reward.

Smurtz and Kline then placed MacBean in their unmarked car and were ready to drive him to a local jail for holding. It was about 10 P.M., and Detective Kline told Smurtz to stop at a package store before heading to the jail. Kline purchased a bottle of Bardolino red wine, Smurtz's favorite. Kline then suggested that they head to the park they'd passed on the way to the funeral home earlier in the day. MacBean began to get a bit nervous, wondering whether he had misjudged these old men in their intent. When they arrived at the park, all three got out of the car and sat on the benches of a nearby picnic table. The park was empty and dimly lit but in a decent neighborhood. All MacBean could think was *Surely they won't hurt me in this kind of place.*

Smurtz then took one handcuff off MacBean and secured it to the bench where they were all sitting. Kline pulled out three plastic cups to pour wine into. MacBean literally sighed.

"Oh my God, Hobo JoJo, you didn't think….?"

"I didn't know what to think!"

"Kline and I just want to celebrate the last crime either of us will solve," said Smurtz.

Kline then added, "Well, JoJo MacBean, I finally got my personal revenge in helping my buddy, Smurtz here, catch you, you being the person who disabled me and all."

"Let me apologize for that, Detective Kline. I surely meant to hurt you but honestly never meant for anything permanent. Guess the adrenaline took over. From the bottom of my heart, I am sorry. Can you still. . .you know?"

"Yes, I can, no thanks to you. What got messed up is my ability to pee straight."

"Hell, old man, I can't pee straight anymore either, and nobody done bopped me with a skillet" said Smurtz laughingly. MacBean tried very hard not to laugh but finally gave in once Kline, himself, started laughing.

"It's not funny at all, it's a goddamned nuisance. But I got money added to my pension for it, so I can't grouse too much. Except for the pain, MacBean. The pain was awful for about six months."

"I'd say you're free to sue me, but right now, I don't have any money. How about I promise to pay you something if I ever have any. What do you think is fair?"

Kline and Smurtz looked at each other, wondering who the hell is this guy anyway? How did a man become so full of such contradictory behavior? Was he a good guy, bad guy, in-between guy, was he crooked, crazy, or just confused?

"I'd say if you gave one hundred thousand to my grandson, I'd be happy," said Kline.

"Don't seem fair that I don't get something for my pain and suffering. It was purely emotional, but I took a lot of ribbing once the truth came out," Smurtz chimed in.

The three men looked at one another and burst out again in another round of laughing. MacBean then held out his hand to Kline. "Deal. If I ever have a hundred thousand, I'll give it to your grandson." Kline took his hand and shook it firmly. "Sorry, Smurtz, but if I have to give him all that money, it's unlikely there'll be anything left over. I'm not a young man either you know."

"Don't worry, I'm really just glad this case is over." As the two old detectives were enjoying the moment, sipping their wine slowly, Kline asked MacBean why he wasn't drinking his wine. He explained that alcohol was a challenge for him, and he hadn't been able to drink red wine anyway since his wife, Maria, died.

It was close to midnight. Neither detective seemed tired enough to fall asleep because of all the excitement still flowing through their veins. Smurtz said to Kline, "is there no way to get some of that reward money?"

"Honestly, I don't think so, Fred. I mean maybe if you asked them, but my hands are tied, I was engaged by the FBI. And I engaged you, which makes you kind of engaged by them, too. The reward doesn't really matter to me, I get by pretty comfortably myself. Besides, damned if I don't think we got a lot more out of this case than mere money. I mean, think about it, Fred. This was one hell of a hard case, but we figured it out. It didn't involve a killer or a psychopath or anybody that stole a ton of money."

"And by God, it was fun!" Old Fred Smurtz then gave MacBean a bear hug. *How lucky can a man get, to always be getting bear hugs from great men. Some rich, some poor, but all of them clearly special.*

"Tell me about some of the other cases you two worked on," said MacBean.

For the next two hours, the detectives regaled MacBean with tales of cops and robbers such as MacBean had never heard.

"But we never had this much fun. Everybody knew what you were doing was wrong, but it didn't feel wrong, you know, guess cause it didn't really involve life or death."

"Well, actually" said MacBean "it did involve death, or at least, the dead."

"That it did. But it brought me back to life. Damned if I don't think I could keep going! How about you?" Smurtz said to Kline.

"The two of you should write a book about your careers. It would make a great story. You guys are real heroes, the kind nobody ever hears about. You faced death many times in bringing guys to justice. And now Hobo JoJo for your ending!" said MacBean.

"Us? It's you who should write a book. Seriously, MacBean, it would give you something to do in prison, if you can't beat this rap," said Kline.

"Kline, I was thinking buddy, what harm has MacBean really done? What good would it be for him to waste away in jail on our tax dollars. Those clients were all filthy rich! And this guy made 'em even richer. And it sure seems like the guy has also learned to help other people less fortunate. Nobody had anything bad to say about the guy, except the ones who knew him when he was really young. And even then, all they said was he was kind of oblivious to the rest of the world. Not the worst thing that can be said about somebody."

"Oh, but Detective Smurtz, it's a terrible thing not to understand other people. It makes you very shallow. Just because you aren't aware you've hurt someone or that someone is hurting, that doesn't make them hurt any less."

"You're being too hard on yourself, so many of your former clients loved you, they said so" Smurtz said.

"I believe they think they did. But they didn't really know me. It was the money I made them that they loved, not the man who made it."

"Maybe. But not a one didn't say how badly they felt about your wife. And it was sincere, too. I've learned to tell when it's real."

MacBean broke down, and the detectives realized just

how much Maria's death had changed this man and left him with a wound that would never fully heal. And, yet, the two detectives also knew that MacBean's journey of the past few years had also changed him and that he was no longer the man who gauged his value according to the bottom line of a bank account.

Detective Kline opened up his briefcase and took a second bottle of the Italian red out of his case. Kline filled the two empty plastic cups and toasted detective Smurtz. "Heck, MacBean," Kline stated "most of the people over sixty years old have known JoJo MacBean through the media sources. And that is a long time! From one of the best businessmen that we have ever known to a homeless person, you're one of a kind. And with these funeral home capers, you had more publicity in your life than most presidents!"

MacBean felt touched by what they said. Thanks, guys, but it wasn't all it's cracked up to be. Outside of my parents, Maria was the only one that made me a happy person. It really took too long for me to find out that all the money in the world doesn't really matter. The more I made, the more I spent, trying to drown my unhappiness with all that money. But it was never enough. I wasted millions of dollars, and then Maria was gone. I suffered a nervous breakdown and the great JoJo MacBean was no more. That's when I realized I couldn't handle, I didn't want to handle, the pressures of maintaining a rich and famous lifestyle anymore. Then I started to drift around the USA shortly after I was released from the hospital. I learned that being homeless is no joke. But I can honestly say I enjoyed drifting around the country without any more business pressure.

"It's not easy feeling sorry for someone who once was a multi-millionaire. And maybe "feeling sorry" aren't the right words," said Kline.

"Yeah, I think it's more that we understand the reason for everything you've done, chimed in Smurtz.

MacBean chuckled "Maybe you can explain it all to me!"

"We don't need to, you know it all yourself," said Kline.

"When it comes to myself, I'm not a quick learner; that's for sure."

"MacBean, nobody's quick when it comes to himself. But how many people try, I mean really try, to find themselves, make a conscious effort to figure out what went wrong. I'll tell you how many, near zero. But you did."

"I guess I discovered we're all on a journey of one sort or another. Each journey is different, but we're all looking for the same thing – some kind of understanding of what makes us tick as humans, and what makes us tick as individuals. I think I figured out a lot of what makes humans tick but not sure I learned much of what makes JoJo MacBean tick."

"You're still not getting it," said Smurtz.

"Maybe I'm not either," added Kline.

"What makes a human tick, and what makes JoJo MacBean tick. . . "Smurtz began.

"Aren't any different, are they?" interrupted MacBean. "I'm only human. To understand one is to understand the other, isn't it?"

"Bingo." Smurtz said with a big grin.

"Smurtz, you've got a lot going on in that noggin of yours," Kline said.

"You listen to me," said Smurtz, "You brought a lot of joy into many people's lives with those capers. But you did it for the game, because we all love a good game."

"And at KBL, I thought it was the money I wanted, but it was the game, it was all one giant game for me."

Smurtz then looked at Kline and said, "Well buddy, our careers are now over, and I think. . ." and then hesitated.

"You thinking what I'm thinking?" responded Kline. At that, both detectives stood up and walked a few feet away from MacBean for a private talk.

"Yep, we should let Hobo JoJo go. Hell, the rest of the

world will think we're the bad guys if we turn him in."

"He didn't kill anyone; no former clients ever pressed any charges against him. The funeral homes want this forgotten as soon as possible, all's left is KBL with the beef about that stupid client list. But considering how much money he made for KBL, it's not going to be good public relations for KBL to go after him."

"You're forgetting the FBI; they always want their man."

"Hell, Kline, even if the Feds get mad at us for releasing JoJo, what can they do to us two old men? By the way, think of all the court time, and the money that would be wasted. Besides, we can say he escaped!" The two men walked back to where MacBean sat.

Kline then looked MacBean in the eye and said, "If we let you go, do you promise you will never do anything like this again? You're a smart man, and I must say smarter than either of us. You still got time to do something good with that mind of yours."

MacBean then replied to Kline, "Look guys, I am not as smart as you think. Look at all the mistakes I made along the way."

"But you learned from them," Smurtz stated.

MacBean then told them, "I promise, you two fine detectives, that I will not pull off any more of these capers. You caught me, and you treated me very well tonight. I really do appreciate your kindness. No more break-ins," MacBean said as he smiled. Smurtz unlocked the handcuffs, and then MacBean hugged both Smurtz and Kline. "But I'm not running away. I don't want to play hide and seek with the FBI the rest of my life. I want to take what's coming to me, and I also want to be able to do some of that good you're saying I'm capable of. Can't do much good if I can't be heard or seen for fear of the FBI."

"But you can't do it from prison, either!" said Kline.

"Not true. There's a better chance of doing good from prison than there would be of doing some good while trying to hide from the world. No, I want you to take me in, and I'll take my medicine from the FBI and from KBL."

"I got a better idea. Best scenario is for you to turn yourself in. The two of us will say we came close to getting you, but you managed to give us the slip."

"You'd do that for me? I mean, you both have stellar records, I'll always be 'the one who got away'."

"We know that. But what have we been talking about tonight, if not doing what's right, not what's easiest?" said Smurtz. Kline put his hand out palm down, Smurtz placed his hand palm down on top of Kline's, and MacBean then placed both his hands-on top.

MacBean and the two old detectives drove to the FBI office in Sacramento. A couple miles from that field office, MacBean exited the car and started walking, eventually reaching the office. As he climbed the first few steps, he saw the detectives' car following him, and he turned around and waved to them as they drove away. He climbed the rest of the steps and turned himself in. As MacBean walked in, there flashed into his mind all the people who had made this walk possible for him: Mum and Dad, Mr. Bloomberg, Sam Slade, Harvey Bernstein, Maria's father, Maria, Rivers, Baldy, Kline, and Smurtz. *God bless their souls!*

The movement Occupy Wall Street emerged in September 2011, primarily as a protest of corporate greed.

6

MAKING A COMEBACK
2009-2012

The market began in 2009 at 9034 and ended 2012 at 12217.

The newspapers and media were on fire with the news that Hobo JoJo had turned himself in. KBL did press charges for the theft of the client list but were willing to allow the punishment to fit the crime. MacBean could never again be a broker anywhere, and he would have to make restitution to any former clients who wished him to do so. Not a single client wished him to. The judge also ordered that MacBean do one hundred hours of community service, which MacBean was only too willing to do, as he was intending to do so in any case. When he flew back to New York City, Rivers was waiting for him at the airport, along with a mob of news media. She had to struggle to reach him, but when she did, the flashes were blinding, and around the world went the picture of Hobo JoJo and his girlfriend hugging and kissing with the headline "Hobo JoJo Returns Home." And that was exactly how MacBean felt, not only for being in NYC but for being in the arms of Rivers. I'm home, I'm finally home.

For the first four months, he turned down all of the offers to tell his story in the media and any speaking engagements while he and Rivers figured out just how to accomplish what needed to be.

Once plans were set, MacBean visited his old homestead, where he was greeted by his tenant, Dave. MacBean gave Dave a choice of allowing MacBean to have an office in the homestead while Dave continued to rent, or to allow MacBean to find Dave another house to rent with MacBean making up any difference in rent for the next twelve months Dave chose to stay in the house, and MacBean also lowered Dave's rent since he was now sharing the house.

The next day MacBean applied for his social security. He figured he could use that for medical and utilities, while he worked on implementing his long-range plan. Of course, the rent was still going into the frozen irrevocable trust and always would be. But MacBean's plan didn't need the house for anything other than as the office for the foundation he would be setting up soon: the MacDyer Fontana Foundation, dedicated to helping those in need. MacBean envisioned it to encompass three main projects. The first would be "Baldy's Eats", a nation-wide effort to create small cafes and diners operated and run by previously homeless veterans. He would partner with Sam's Foundation who helped find housing for veterans. *I hope somehow you know now that's the reason we met, Baldy.* They would be trained as cooks and/or managers and would cycle into other similar jobs after twelve months at a "Baldy's Eats". The second was to create a grant program for any community to apply for funds for mental health counselors who would literally live amongst the homeless. The third was just for MacBean and Rivers. The Foundation would purchase Bloomberg's Deli, which had been replaced by a hamburg joint for several years before being closed altogether. It would be restored to its retro glory, and operated as a nonprofit, with any profits realized donated to children's out of school educational programs, with a special curriculum for young entrepreneurs that JoJo MacBean co-designed with an educator.

After the four months of media hiatus, and with their plan in place, Rivers and MacBean embarked on a nation-wide speaking tour, earning good fees that would support the building of their Foundation. MacBean also asked KBL if they would consider allowing him to canvas by mail his former clients to ask for their financial assistance. KBL was very reluctant but also knew that MacBean had the media eating out of his hand, so quick agreement was ultimately going to be in KBL's interest. MacBean also asked specific clients to be on the Board of the Foundation, helping to ensure even larger donations. By the end of the year, the Foundation had amassed enough funding to support several "Baldy's Eats". By the end of the second year, the Bloomberg's 501c3 Deli opened to great fanfare with the NYC mayor cutting the ribbon.

Colleges and Fortune 500 companies throughout the world were calling MacBean to book speaking engagements. Being the former businessman that he was, JoJo did a little research on pricing these events. He set a high fee of five thousand for radio interviews, ten for TV talk shows, and twenty-five thousand for lectures at a college or a Fortune 500 company. Of course, the networks and the speaking engagements were covered by a sponsor for each event. At the end of 2010, MacBean finally accepted a million-dollar advance, after taxes, for a book about his life, plus a percentage of the royalties from the book. The million minus one hundred thousand went directly into the Foundation, and royalties would help support MacBean and Rivers. The one hundred thousand went to Kline's grandson. Averaging about a hundred and twenty lectures and interviews a year, MacBean and the Foundation were on solid ground by the end of year two.

In 2011, MacBean even gave a graduation speech to the students of Harvard University, one of only a few speeches each year he granted without any fee. He continued to function as a Board member of the Foundation. His tenant, Dave, eventually married and moved to his fiancée's much larger house, and MacBean and Rivers moved into the old homestead full time. They never planned to marry. MacBean felt his track record was so poor it would only spoil the deep friendship and love between them. Rivers made him change his mind when she announced that she wanted to adopt a child she had met in her own volunteer work at a children's hospital. MacBean had no objection but felt that even though adoption agencies were far more lenient than they used to be in regards to single parent adoptions, every child deserved two parents, if at all possible. The two married in 2012, and shortly thereafter, in 2013, a twelve-year old boy named Jonathan Jones joined them. The young boy was smart as a whip but confined to a wheelchair with a degenerative disease that would someday end his life too soon. As his present to MacBean the first Christmas with them, he asked to be called JoJo Jr. after his dad. That same first Christmas, MacBean gave JoJo Jr. a present of Sweet Sammy's Cleveland Indians baseball cap, along with the story of that night.

MacBean ended his story saying, "Now I hope you'll understand this, JoJo, but when I die, hopefully not for quite a while, I have to take the cap with me cause I promised to bring it back." The young boy laughed, and they smiled at each other, both knowing full well that the odds were that JoJo Jr. would precede JoJo Sr. In all his travels across the country MacBean thought he had never met a human being with greater courage than this extraordinary young man.

The homeless guys that JoJo ran into during his "hobo" years were bragging about once meeting him. MacBean had visited Abraham, Mohammed, and Jesús and offered each of them an opportunity to be employees at "Baldy's Eats" around the country, sort of "roving ambassadors" for MacBean. MacBean found Abraham too ill for a job, but he helped him find and pay for a good doctor. Mohammed was happy at his paying job at a food bank in Minnesota. Jesús had also found a solid job after getting into a training program to become a certified nurse's assistant, but he did help a couple of other homeless vets find their way to a "Baldy's Eats".

MacBean did not bring up detectives Kline and Smurtz by name in his lectures. He never wanted to take the chance of getting the detectives into hot water, so he always said he gave himself up and never specifically mentioned their names. About five years had gone by when MacBean read of Kline's passing. He called Smurtz and asked whether or not he should break his promise to the detectives and break into the funeral home to switch clothes with Kline. Smurtz then laughed and said, "MacBean, just before he died, that's exactly what Kline said to me, laughing about it the same way you are!" MacBean did attend the services for Kline, as he also did for Smurtz less than a year later. He hoped he still had time to edit his book before it went to press, now being able to tell the full truth.

He did have time, and the full story was told. The story of a young man gifted with a talent not for mathematics and business so much as for playing "games' with those talents. The story of a man who had one goal in life that he had thought was to make money by playing games. The story of a man who had no idea that love actually required some sacrifices. The story of a man who felt he had a story to tell others, but actually needed to hear the story of those others. The story of a man who was born and raised, who conquered Wall Street, who was conquered by Wall Street, who lived a "hobo" life, who stole from dead people, and who made a comeback. But really, it was just the story of a man who found his humanity, a man who became a human MacBean.

THE END

P.S. *I, Rivers Fitzpatrick, have written this book from the notes of MacBean and Baldy, and conversations with MacBean. As he always says, "It's all truth, even the parts that might not be true."*

Rules for Knuckleheads like JoJo MacBean
Never take – anyone or anything – for granted. Ever.

1.
WORK HARD
If you don't care enough to work hard,
why should anyone else?

2.
WORK PASSIONATELY
You should have a fire in your belly to be the
best you can be, otherwise why bother?

3.
WORK SMART
Just like school – do your homework and never
stop learning. Be as smart with your time as you
are with your money.

4.
WORK KIND
Recognize that your job as a human is to serve
everybody: not just clients, but employees; not just
loved ones but your community; not just those easy
to love but those who need love most.
Love is unconditional, but it is not acceptance of
that which should be changed.

5.
WORK HUMBLE
As the saying goes – keep your words soft and
tender today for tomorrow you may have
to eat them.

FOOTNOTES

Items considered common knowledge and quotes that can be easily located on the web have not been footnoted.

1. Wikipedia: Wall Street Bombing @ https://en.wikipedia.org/wiki/Wall_Street_bombing

2. This and all other stock quotes provided are from: Dow Jones Industrial Average History @ http://www.fedprimerate.com/dow-jones-industrial-average-history-djia.htm

3. Wall Street History Timeline @ https://www.history.com/topics/us-states/wall-street-timeline

4. Haaretz @ https://www.haaretz.com/us-news/.premium.MAGAZINE-new-deli-the- rise-and-fall-and-rise-of-the-old-n-y-jewish-deli-1.5730860

5. CNNBusiness, Bull Markets Through History @ https://www.cnn.com › 2019/04/23 ›

6. USA Today Nov. 21, 2013 online @ https://www.usatoday.com/story/money/markets/2013/11/21/stock-market-reaction-to-jfk-assassination/3662171/

7. The Scotsman, Great Quotes on Scottish Life @ https://www.scotsman.com/200voices/thinkers/great-scottish-quotes-life/

8. The Electrical Worker 1914/May 233/1: via QUORA @ https://www.quora.com/Where-did-the-saying-its-not-what-you-know-but-who-you-know-originate

9. Wall St. History Timeline @ https://www.history.com/topics/us-states/wall-street-timeline

10. Wall Street Journal, June 15, 2009, Is This Bull Cyclical or Secular? @https://www.wsj.com › articles

11. PassItOn.com, Napoleon Hill quotes.

12. Wise Old Sayings @http://www.wiseoldsayings.com/role-models-quotes/

13. PBS WGBH The American Experience, Dow Jones Chemical Co.@https://www.pbs.org/wgbh/americanexperience/features/two-days-in-october-dow-chemical-and-use-napalm/

14. Wikepedia: Nixon Shock @ https://en.wikipedia.org/wiki/Nixon_shock

15. Wikepedia: 1973-74 Stock Market Crash @ https://en.wikipedia.org/wiki/1973–74_stock_market_crash

16. Wikipedia: History of Apple Inc. @ https://en.wikipedia.org/wiki/History_of_Apple_Inc.

17. Wikipedia: History of Microsoft @ https://en.wikipedia.org/wiki/History_of_Microsoft

18. Wall St. Timeline @ https://www.history.com/topics/us-states/wall-street-timeline

19. CNN.com @ https://www.cnn.com/2013/11/05/us/1993-world-trade-center-bombing-fast-facts/index.html

20. 1990s Flashback @ www.1990sflashback.com › 1996 › economy

21. Wikipedia: September 11 Attacks @https://en.wikipedia.org › wiki › September_11_attacks

22. Wikipedia: Hobo @ https://en.wikipedia.org/wiki/Hobo

23. The Washington Post, Aug. 18, 2014, @ https://www.washingtonpost.com › local 2014/08/18

24. Wall Street Timeline @ https://www.history.com/topics/us-states/wall-street-timeline